In 1965, the Council for Basic Education sponsored the writing of *The Miseducation of American Teachers*. This book, written by James D. Koerner, was and continues to be an influential examination of the intellectually vacuous preparation given the nation's teaching force. Thirty years later and the general tenor of teacher education has changed little. However, we now have some reason to hope for something better.

Into this context comes Harriet Tyson's book, *Who Will Teach the Children?*, once again sponsored by the Council. Tyson has located teacher preparation programs that strive to be both academically rigorous and pedagogically sound. What makes these programs work and what interferes with the fulfillment of their good intentions are the heart and substance of this valuable book.

Good teacher education, unfortunately, continues to be a rarity among the mundane. It is my sincere wish that this book will provide the antidote to further miseducation in this vital profession.

A. Graham Down
President
Council for Basic Education

WHO
Will
TEACH
the
CHILDREN?

HARRIET TYSON

*Sponsored by
the Council for
Basic Education*

WHO
Will
TEACH
the
CHILDREN?

Progress and Resistance in Teacher Education

Jossey-Bass Publishers · San Francisco

Substantial discounts on bulk quantities of Jossey-Bass books are available to corporations, professional associations, and other organizations. For details and discount information, contact the special sales department at Jossey-Bass Inc., Publishers. (415) 433-1740; Fax (415) 433-0499.

For sales outside the United States, contact Maxwell Macmillan International Publishing Group, 866 Third Avenue, New York, New York 10022.

Manufactured in the United States of America. Nearly all Jossey-Bass books and jackets are printed on recycled paper containing at least 10 percent postconsumer waste, and many are printed with either soy- or vegetable-based ink, which emits fewer volatile organic compounds during the printing process than petroleum-based ink.

Library of Congress Cataloging-in-Publication Data

Tyson, Harriet.
  Who will teach the children? : progress and resistance in teacher education / Harriet Tyson.
      p.   cm.—(The Jossey-Bass education series) (The Jossey-Bass higher and adult education series)
  Includes bibliographical references and index.
  ISBN 1-55542-600-X
  1. Teachers—Training of—United States.   2. Education—Study and teaching (Higher)—United States.   I. Title.   II. Series.
LB1715.T97   1994
370.71'0973—dc20   93-36595
                                                                  CIP

FIRST EDITION
HB Printing   10 9 8 7 6 5 4 3 2 1   *Code 9407*

CONTENTS

Part Two: Obstacles to Reform

Part Three: Prospects for the Future

PREFACE

It would be hard to find a highly educated adult in the United States today who lacks an opinion, nearly always a negative one, about the education of American teachers. For example, I recently had a conversation with an acquaintance I had not seen since 1980, when he retired after thirty years of service in the U.S. Department of Education. This is how the conversation went.

"What are you up to these days?" he asked.

"I'm writing a book about teacher education."

"What a boring topic!"

"I don't think so," I said. "I'm interested in how teachers learn subject matter, or don't learn it, and how they learn to put it across."

"*That's* not teacher education!" he hissed. "It's all those damned methods courses."

"All states require a bunch of liberal arts courses," I said, "and most require a subject matter major—in addition to what you call teacher education. They don't study their calculus or history in the ed school, you know."

"The whole thing is a mess," he said, shifting ground. "Some people major in education, some get a regular degree and then a master's in teaching, and some people just go straight into the classroom. There's *no* pattern!" he said, as if we were discussing the dangers posed by a lack of uniformity in the design of nuclear power plants. "Teachers ought to do what lawyers and doctors do.

They take their degrees in the liberal arts *first,*" he said emphatically. "*Then* they go to professional school."

"Where they will take all those horrible methods courses?" I asked him.

He shrugged.

"Doctors and lawyers get liberal arts degrees to become nice, well-rounded people, but what they learn isn't directly related to what they *do* in the practice of medicine or law," I said. "For teachers, the liberal arts are the tools of the trade, the stuff they will teach."

"It's all those damn *methods* courses," he said, returning to his original point. "They're a bunch of crap!"

"That's not what I heard from the beginning teachers I've been interviewing. Have you talked to anybody under thirty about it?"

"No, I don't even know anybody under thirty."

Harold's opinions are not made up of the whole cloth. There is a long history of cream puff "methods" courses, and many practicing teachers who were forced to endure such courses disparage them to anyone who will listen. Also, there are "foundations" courses (the history, philosophy, and sociology of education), which many teachers dismiss as "just theory," by which they mean the courses are impractical and unrelated to their work as teachers. A strong case actually can be made that systematic study of the foundations of education is intensely practical, if only for the purpose of inoculating teachers against recurring fads. The fact remains, however, that these courses are usually taught in ways that obscure their practicality. The methods courses that are thin gruel, as well as the foundations courses that are badly taught to unappreciative students, still exist and continue to supply fodder to critics of schools of education.

Negative views of teacher education and teachers are grounded in both personal experience and widely disseminated information. Frank Murray and Daniel Fallon summarize the public's view of teacher education and teachers as of 1980, when a flurry of education reform reports hit the street:

The problem with teaching is that the wrong people
are studying the wrong things in the wrong places.
They are the wrong people because there is an over-
representation of low-scorers on any credible test of
intellectual accomplishment. Nearly 40 percent of the
bottom 20 percent of scorers on the standardized college aptitude tests are enrolled in teacher education,
for example. Prospective teachers seem to be people
who have, for whatever reasons, few other options for
white collar work. Moreover, teachers study the wrong
things. They study too much pedagogy, a field that at
best has slight claim to a scholarly base of knowledge,
and they study too little of the disciplines that are, by
contrast, well-grounded in long-standing traditions of
scholarly work and substance. Finally, too much of
the work is done in the wrong place—in the ivory
tower—not in field sites where there are clinical opportunities to validate and practice what has been
learned in the college classroom.[1]

These Harold-like opinions are becoming dated. The univer-
sally condemned methods courses are now mixed with new courses
in schools of education and with tightly correlated internships in
schools that tax the full array of human capacities. Since 1980,
widespread discontent over teacher education has brought about
widely supported proposals for change, as well as actual changes in
state laws and university policies.

The most popular remedies have been the following:

- To require higher academic standards for entrance into and exit
  from schools of education
- To abolish the undergraduate major for elementary teachers
  (with few exceptions, secondary teachers have always taken degrees in the subjects they planned to teach)
- To set limits on the number of education courses that can be
  required of future teachers
- To lengthen teacher training so that courses in pedagogy will

not come at the expense of liberal arts studies or upper-division courses in the student's major field of study

- To require future teachers to spend more time in the schools, learning their craft from experienced teachers

One or more of these remedies have been put into place in the overwhelming majority of today's teacher education schools.[2]

But are these popular remedies based on correct analyses of the problems? Will they improve the quality of teachers and teaching in the nation's schools? The examination of these questions is one of the major purposes of this book.

Teacher education does not begin with enrollment in a college and does not end with graduation and certification. Whatever prospective teachers have absorbed in twelve or more years of elementary and secondary schooling and four or more years of college is modified—sometimes obliterated—by their early experiences as student teachers, interns, and beginning teachers. Therefore *teacher education,* as it will be considered in this book, includes whatever attitudes, capacities, and understanding prospective teachers brought with them to college; the influence of the first year on the job and the trauma that is the lot of most beginning teachers; and the early years of teaching, when teachers begin to resist, succumb to, or flee from the system as we know it.

Equally important, but beyond the scope of this book, is the experience of teachers over the span of their careers. Depending on how they are treated, they continue to learn, or they do not. They refine their teaching skills, or they do not. If people in authority do not care about whether teachers keep up with their disciplines, but merely expect teachers to keep students under control, "implement" curricula designed by higher-ups, "teach" from wretched textbooks, and prepare the kids for low-level tests, then all but the most glorious of teachers will probably stop growing and learning at some point.

The reform of teacher education can be considered only in relation to some vision of what it ought to be, some yardstick against which its current effectiveness is being measured. For the purposes of this book, the yardstick is whether the children taught by graduates of teacher education programs can *understand* as well as memorize, *apply* as well as state, *imagine* as well as copy, *solve* problems rather than shrug them off, and *make themselves felt* in a society that seems to be falling apart for lack of these capacities.

In our schools, teachers historically have taught by lecture and pupils have learned (*if* they learned) by rote. In families where the bonds of love and visions of the good life have kept children's noses to the grindstone, the children have been able to persist through meaningless drudgery until meaning at last emerges. They have been able to fashion the bits and pieces of a fragmented curriculum into a whole that can be called an education. Children who have been unable to do so have fallen by the academic wayside.

In the long history of schooling, there are few exceptions to the pattern of rote learning and widespread failure. Socrates tried something else, and we all know what happened to him. Some of the great schoolmasters of the Renaissance taught for understanding, but they enjoyed the moral authority of the Church; they felt free to speak sternly about childrearing to the parents of their students and to maintain standards in the face of parental resistance. John Dewey's Progressive Education, which sought to teach everybody to understand and apply knowledge, lasted only briefly. It was brought down by a wave of immigration in the 1920s and 1930s that swamped the schools, and by the excesses of those who misconstrued Dewey's ideas. Those business leaders who wanted a mass of obedient workers rather than independent thinkers sometimes also resisted Dewey's movement. Then as now, many believed that ordinary teachers and students were not capable of a more rigorous education.

Now, though, arguments for a more challenging, coherent, and applied education, and assessments of who will be able to benefit from it, have changed. It is increasingly evident that even many bright and affluent students no longer respond to the test-driven, shallow curriculum (mostly mandated by politicians and distant bureaucrats), or to formula-driven teaching (mostly mandated by misguided and cheaply gotten-up teacher evaluation systems). Even many "good" students don't see the point of it all, don't remember what they have learned by rote, and are not willing to work very hard in school. And the current approach to curriculum and teaching utterly fails the "forgotten half"—the students who are not going to college.

The case for educating everyone is compelling. Most other advanced nations—our economic competitors—do it far better than we do. We *must* do it: we need a better-educated, more civilized population if our form of government is to survive. We must do it because we are not a nation that permits people to starve on the streets, and yet we cannot afford to subsidize the housing and feeding of increasing numbers of unemployed and unemployable people. Profound and dimly understood changes in technology, in the domestic and world economies, and in the interdependence of people all over the world make this kind of shift in goals and pedagogy a necessity for survival. Achieving these goals depends heavily (but not exclusively) on the nation's teachers and on those who educate them, license them, hire them, lead them, and determine their salaries and working conditions.

Two decades of fruitful research on teaching and learning make teaching for understanding and teaching everybody appear more feasible than in the past. This new knowledge is still spotty, however. It is also contaminated by some of the same old drivel, newly recycled, that has long discredited pedagogy as a field of study. Nevertheless, much of the new knowledge about teaching and learning, especially in mathematics and science, is as solid and intellectually challenging as any material offered in the academic disciplines.

Everyone can't learn everything to the same level of complexity, but there is ample reason to believe that virtually all students can learn much more than they do now. That statement has been made before by optimists in each wave of educational reform; sometimes it is merely cheerleading. But this time there is more evidence than ever before that it is true, and there are more sophisticated tools for making it a reality.

It may be that radically reformed teacher education and teacher practice, aimed at deeper, more thoughtful, and more applicable education, is still beyond our grasp. The weight of institutions—colleges, school bureaucracies, teacher unions, testing companies, state legislatures—is heavy and often tips us in the opposite direction. Even the best-educated, most carefully trained teachers are apt to be crushed in a system that is decidedly inhospitable to what they know and can do. Nevertheless, the goal of training teachers for a new kind of practice—devoted to students' depth of understanding, to their ability to use what they know in the world, and to their capacity to learn on their own—is worth striving for.

Can we be a little more patient than in the past? Can we begin to believe the evidence that poor and minority students can and do succeed in challenging school programs? Can educators take care in the way they talk to laymen? Can legislators and administrators resist the temptation to convert half-understood ideas into uniform requirements? Can the public be persuaded that the investment is worth it? If so, we may yet wrench education out of the nineteenth century and into the twenty-first. Even when there are political and economic setbacks along the road, we may yet be wise enough to rachet some fundamental improvements in the quality of teachers and teaching and in the school experience of the vast majority of the nation's children.

Background and Contents of This Book

To gather material for this book, I read through most of the major books published over the past fifty years on the subject of teacher education reform. After that, I selected for study five schools of education and one entire state, places said to be doing good things in teacher education reform. I was not disappointed. Although in every one of these places I saw signs of the old problems that have dogged the enterprise for a century, I also saw evidence of new energy and intellectual rigor in teacher education programs. I also found a new breed of teacher educators, people who hear the urgency in the calls for reform and who are making prodigious personal sacrifices to bring about change.

Chapter One explores the poverty of both curriculum and teaching in most undergraduate arts and science courses. It challenges the popular myth that teachers would teach better if only they took more courses (as currently taught) in the academic disciplines. Chapters Two through Seven in Part One are portraits of teacher education in the places I visited. The names of the individuals have been changed. Chapter Eight envisages an ideal drawn from all the preceding portraits.

Part Two dissects the institutional restraints on reform. Chapter Nine explores obstacles to good teaching posed by schools' systematic disrespect for teachers' subject matter and teaching knowledge and by institutional assaults on teachers' dignity. Chapter Ten shows why the states don't do the job they are presumed to do—protect the public from unqualified teachers. States have a conflict of interest: as employers, they prefer cheap and plentiful teachers to good ones.

Part Three assesses the chances for serious reform of teacher education and teaching. Chapter Eleven examines whether American business really wants reform and is willing to pay for it. School bureaucracies, teacher unions, and the upper middle class are portrayed as unconstructive players; working-class parents are seen as the strongest potential allies of school reformers. There may be a lack of broad popular support for reform, but other forces are at work that will goad universities and schools into better performance, even without popular uprisings. Chapter Twelve foresees the inevitable reform of teacher education and teaching. Predictable forces will converge over the next decade: changes in the composition of the teaching force, continued pressure on teachers to improve educational outcomes, teachers' discovery of their own knowledge and skills in restructured schools, a decline in the size of school bureaucracies, and a shift in the ethos of teacher unions. There will come a moment when a critical mass of better-educated, more assertive teachers—as individuals, in small groups, in faculties, as members of disciplinary organizations, and as union members—becomes a positive force in the reform of teacher education and in teachers' own emergence as members of a respected, learned profession.

Washington, D.C.   Harriet Tyson
November 1993

ACKNOWLEDGMENTS

I want to thank William H. Willcox, a very literary lawyer who is not only my husband but also a masterful editor.

I thank Amy Rukea Stempel, formerly of the Council for Basic Education and now a teacher in India, who helped me amass and digest mountains of information, and who also wrote an excellent chapter which, alas, ended up on the cutting-room floor.

I thank Stephanie Soper of the Council for Basic Education, whose combination of knowledge, quick-wittedness, taste, and facility with computers rescued me from countless errors and contributed to a polished manuscript.

Patte Barth, editor of *Basic Education,* continually offered critiques and insights and sometimes supplied magic words.

The Lilly Endowment, Inc., the Katherine Mabis McKenna Foundation, Inc., the Smith Richardson Foundation, Inc., and the Sarah Scaife Foundation supported the development of this book with their generous contributions, and I am grateful.

I am also grateful to my publisher, Jossey-Bass, for accepting this project, and to Lesley Iura, who managed the project with an artful combination of directness and diplomacy.

THE AUTHOR

HARRIET TYSON received her B.A. degree (1953) from George Washington University in foreign affairs and did graduate work in education and psychology at the University of Maryland (1959).

Tyson has taught history and art and served as an elected member and president of the board of education of Montgomery County, Maryland, from 1972 to 1976. During the heyday of federal activity in public education, she was director of the Educational Staff Seminar, a Ford Foundation–sponsored seminar program for senior federal education policy makers. She has worked as a reporter, writer, editor, researcher, or project director for a variety of Washington-based organizations, including the Institute for Educational Leadership, the Council for Basic Education, the Association for Supervision and Curriculum Development, the Council of Chief State School Officers, the National Center for Improving Science Education, and the National Board for Professional Teaching Standards. She worked as a researcher for the RAND Corporation's Center for the Study of the Teaching Profession and coauthored the RAND report *Case Studies for Teacher Evaluation: A Study of Effective Practices* (1984, with A. Wise, L. Darling-Hammond, and M. McLaughlin).

After she directed a national study of American textbooks, Tyson wrote *A Conspiracy of Good Intentions: America's Textbook Fiasco,* published by the Council for Basic Education (1988). Her other published works include *Reforming Science Education/Restructuring the Public Schools: Roles for the Scientific Community* (Occasional Paper, Institute for Educational Leadership, 1990),

"The Texas Teacher Evaluation System: What Does It Really Measure?" (*American Educator*, Spring 1987), "The Values Vacuum: A Provocative Explanation for Parental Discontent" (*American Educator*, Fall 1987), and "The Great Textbook Machine and Prospects for Reform" (*Social Education*, January 1986).

WHO
Will
TEACH
the
CHILDREN?

1

The Subject Matters, But the Academics Just Don't Get It

The most profound obstacle to good teacher education and good teaching is the poverty of teaching and curriculum in undergraduate arts and sciences departments in the United States. Great college teachers happen by accident, not because the system helps them be good teachers or rewards them if they are. Teaching an academic subject as though the students could wait ten years to put all the pieces together does not work very well for anybody, but it is even less helpful to those who will become the nation's teachers. Here is some evidence of what teachers need to know and are not getting from their academic studies.

It has been fashionable for decades to shudder at the academic bankruptcy of "ed schools" and to be outraged that "all those methods courses" steal too much college time away from studies in the academic disciplines. Much of the finger-pointing at teacher education has been done by arts and sciences professors in the very universities that harbor schools of education. The portraits of schools of education in the chapters that follow, as well as the findings of systematic scholars like John Goodlad, suggest that too many American

1

professors, especially those in science and mathematics, take more delight in scorning teacher education and teachers than in teaching the future teachers in their classes. They do not perceive their own role in perpetuating poor education in the elementary and secondary schools. Virtually every academic I interviewed thought himself an excellent teacher; only a few thought that their own teaching (more often, their colleagues' teaching) could be improved, or that they could learn anything from people who have spent their entire lives studying and practicing the art of teaching.

The battle between subject matter and pedagogy has been going on for a long time, and in each decade the battle has been fought anew. In *Crisis in the Classroom* (1970), Charles Silberman notes once again what critics of teacher education seem perennially to forget: "The high school physics or chemistry teacher typically took his bachelor's degree in physics or chemistry, not education. . . . If he didn't know his chemistry, it was the chemistry department's, not the education department's, fault."[1] In the years since Silberman wrote *Crisis in the Classroom,* profound shifts in the governance and funding of universities, in the reward system for professors, and in the knowledge base for teaching have made the problem of academic insufficiency in subject matter even more acute.

The first shift concerns the flood of federal and corporate funding for university-based research, a development that has diminished the quality of undergraduate education. The glamour of doing research, and the prestige that comes to professors who bring in grant money, has turned heads and hearts away from the humdrum task of teaching mere undergraduates. The rule of "publish or perish" has been applied with increasing fierceness to decisions about who gets tenure or promotion or a pay raise, and college faculty have spent less time and energy teaching and more time in the frantic scramble to publish in scholarly journals. (Some of these seem to exist for the sole purpose of providing enough publication outlets for the numbers of faculty members needing to fatten their résumés.) Far too many academics have come to regard the teaching of undergraduates, and especially the teaching of future teachers, as low-status work to be avoided. In *Killing the Spirit* (1990), Page Smith writes: "Testimony to the bad consciences of universities about the sorry state of the teaching function is the widespread practice of awarding, with much fanfare, cash prizes to the 'teacher-of-the-year.' This is supposed to demonstrate an institution's commitment to 'excellence in teaching.' What it does, in fact, is to distort and demean the true nature of teaching. It is also often the case that the untenured winners of such awards soon disappear from the scene, victims of the publish-or-perish rule."[2]

The second major shift that has occurred since 1970 is that there is now a quite respectable knowledge base about how human beings come to learn subject matter, and about what it takes to teach the subject matter. The ideas of Socrates, John Dewey, and Jerome Bruner still attract the support of those who care about good teaching, but now there is fairly hard evidence that their models are better than the ones we use. Lecturing at passive students works for only a small number of students, yet the professoriate lectures away. Students don't learn very much from textbooks, yet professors assign readings in textbooks, and do so with special enthusiasm if they wrote the books themselves and can earn royalties by forcing their students to buy them. In keeping their distance from pedagogical researchers and public school teachers, academic professors seem to keep themselves ignorant of what they might do to reach many more of their students.

A third major shift, related to the second, is that educational policy makers and industrial leaders are now calling for schools that make use of new knowledge about teaching and learning. It has become morally and economically unacceptable (even though it is still politically acceptable) to fail to educate half the population to the level required for modern life. Thoughtful leaders want changes in the purposes of schooling and in methods of teaching, so that the vast majority of students can be prepared to do something real in the world, rather than pass tests of school-based knowledge. Moreover, they believe such changes are possible. These changes in turn require a new understanding of "knowing," an understanding now somewhat foreign to most of the college professors who teach subject matter to future teachers.

In the face of intense disincentives to good undergraduate teaching, despite new information about the ways in which knowledge in the disciplines needs to be presented to future teachers, and despite public anxiety about the state of American public education, the reformers of the 1980s and 1990s continue to frame the pedagogy/content issue as an either/or proposition and to advocate more courses in subject matter and fewer in pedagogy.

Professors in departments within the arts and sciences usually favor more academic study for teachers, even if some of those professors are not very welcoming to the future teachers who might become members of their classes. They think prospective teachers will fare better in *their* classes than in classes taught by hyphenated professors (for example, science-educators, math-educators). They often refer to their own as "real" courses and to the education school counterparts as "watered down," although it is hard to pin academics down on what that accusation means. They talk of "capstone" courses in the senior year, courses said to help students deeply understand a discipline, but which education majors often miss because they are compelled to take the education courses required for licensure.

But if more course taking led to deeper understanding, and if depth of knowledge made for good teaching, the greatest teachers would be found in universities. Derek Bok, president of Harvard University, comments on poor collegiate teaching: "Faculties *do* seem maddeningly indifferent at times to problems that have been obvious for generations. Medical schools continue to weary first-year students with endless recitations of soon-forgotten details; many science departments still misconceive the idea of general education by forcing non-scientists to take introductory courses designed for future specialists; faculties everywhere cling to the custom of grading papers and exams without returning much in the way of comment to their students."[3] For whatever reason, the most assertive critics of teacher education have ignored the idea, implicit in Bok's lament, that students are not learning subject matter because their professors stubbornly misconstrue and often neglect their own teaching work.

The solution most commonly proposed by recent education reformers has been to support (and, if they have real power, to enact) the requirement that future teachers take either more courses in subject matter or fewer courses in education. Other reformers advocate the abolition of education schools altogether, contending that many of the "brightest and best" would enter teaching if only they did not have to endure the intellectually demeaning courses required by schools of education and/or state licensing authorities. This line of argument, along with teacher shortages in various specialties, has induced thirty-three states to create "alternate route" programs that can (but often do not) provide a little summer training prior to teaching, some on-the-job training under the guidance of mentor teachers (who may or may not be given training or time off to spend with the "alternate route" novice), and perhaps some night courses. It all depends on the state's or the school district's rules. As things have turned out, however, only a fraction of the already small number of "alternate route" teachers have been graduates of highly competitive colleges who were longing to teach but did not want to take education courses. For the most part, those who have entered through the "alternate routes" have had the same middling academic records as the regularly prepared applicants, but they have had much less preparation for teaching work itself.

Whatever the seeming merits of the case for academic emphasis, the push for more courses may turn out to be just one more in a long line of reforms that have exhausted everybody without producing results. New research on the knowledge of majors and nonmajors in various disciplines challenges the presumed cause-and-effect relationship between academic courses and "deep" understanding. This chapter presents some of that research, in the hope that the reader will become a more informed observer of the debate over content versus pedagogy.

Solar System Fantasies

A 1991 videotape produced by Phil Sadler of the Smithsonian Astrophysical Observatory in Cambridge, Massachusetts, opens on the happy occasion of a Harvard University graduation ceremony. An interviewer is posing some elementary scientific questions to faculty members, resplendent in their academic robes and colors, and to new graduates, beaming in their caps and gowns. In answer to the first question—"Why is it warmer in the summer than in the winter?"—virtually everyone says, incorrectly, that the earth is closer to the sun in the summer than in the winter. (Consider that when

Washington, D.C., swelters, Rio de Janeiro is chilly.) When asked to explain the phases of the moon, virtually everyone cheerfully explains that a partial moon occurs when the earth gets between the sun and the moon and casts a shadow. If you are now saying to yourself, "What's the matter with that?" you are a member of a very large but nevertheless mistaken majority.* The video then switches to a junior high science classroom in Brookline, Massachusetts, where a teacher struggles to help her students dislodge the very same misconceptions held by the Harvard celebrants. The teacher has provided simulation equipment to help the students discover their naïve misconceptions and replace them with scientifically correct ideas. Unlike many of her counterparts in college-level physics, though, this teacher *knows* that her students are apt to misunderstand these rather simple propositions, *knows* that their naïve ideas cannot be dispelled by merely telling the students what is true, *knows* how to raise the students' misunderstandings to the surface, and *experiments* with ways to help them confront the conflict between tenacious folk understanding and science. Her energetic and well-informed teaching is only partly successful, though. Some students simply cannot let go of their own ideas. Others fail to internalize what they see demonstrated even in the best models and experiments.

Natural Selection: How the Camel Got His Humph

Beth A. Bishop and Charles W. Anderson studied the degree to which students in a biology course for nonmajors were able to ex-

---

*Two-dimensional diagrams in textbooks have led many people to believe, erroneously, that the earth, moon, and sun move in the same plane, and therefore the earth comes between the other two and casts a shadow. In fact, they *aren't* all in the same plane, and the earth shadows the moon only during the rare eclipse.

Except during an eclipse, the sun always lights an entire hemisphere of the moon. During the full moon we see that. The rest of the time, we see only a portion of the lit part—at first gradually less, and then gradually more. That's because the moon travels around the earth, so its position relative to us changes. As we watch it on successive nights, we can see more or less of its lit and dark parts.

plain, in scientifically acceptable ways, instances of natural selection in nature.[4] One instance was as follows:

> Cheetahs (large African cats) are able to run faster than 60 miles per hour when chasing prey. How would a biologist explain *how* the ability to run fast evolved in cheetahs, assuming their ancestors could only run 20 miles per hour?

On tests before and after instruction in biological evolution, the researchers used this example and others to probe the students' ability to apply principles they had learned in class to situations in nature. Even though all the students had studied biology previously, and more than a third had taken two or more biology courses, fewer than 25 percent of the students gave scientifically correct explanations on the pretest. According to the researchers' results, the amount of the students' previous biology instruction had no effect on their performance on the test, nor did their belief in the truthfulness of the theory of evolution.

The students couldn't distinguish between the two independent processes operating in natural selection: first, that nature throws out random variations among individuals within a population; and second, that as the environment changes, some of those random variations are more helpful than others in the individual battle for survival, and those individuals with the most useful variations are more likely to reproduce themselves, so that the percentage of individuals with useful traits gradually increases over very long periods of time. Collapsing these two processes into one, the students came up with the long-discredited explanation that traits could be developed according to "need" and then inherited by offspring (for example, consider the eternally popular idea that giraffes "developed" long necks because they needed to eat treetop leaves, or that porcupines "developed" quills in order to protect themselves).

Bishop and Anderson used their insights into this and other sources of students' confusion to design a curriculum that would help students acquire a scientific understanding of evolution. But for all their efforts, only half the students showed improved understanding on the posttest. The researchers concluded that "most presently used methods of teaching about evolution by natural selection are ineffective for this population of students" (that is, students in a fairly selective state university).

That an estimated half of the college-educated population fails to understand biological evolution has consequences, say these researchers: "This lack of knowledge reduces the creation/evolution debate to, as creationists argue, a dispute between two different kinds of faith. . . . Most students who believe in the truth of evolution apparently based their belief more on acceptance of the power and prestige of science than on an understanding of the reasoning that had led scientists to their conclusions."

It appears that, in this case, the science-educators were conducting more rigorous science education than their counterparts in a typical college biology department. The professorial tradition, especially in the sciences, is to dish out the information and encourage those who "get it" to become graduate students. Such professors are often impatient with students who don't get it, and few have the skill or will to surface students' misconceptions and design teaching accordingly. The future teachers taught by such professors are likely to repeat the cycle of superficial teaching: a forced march through biological taxonomy, presentation of definitions and procedures, limited laboratory work, and little time spent on "why" questions or Socratic dialogue. The students they teach are likely to repeat the pattern of quickly forgetting facts and memorizing definitions without understanding their meaning. Chances are they will be unaware, like the Harvard professors and graduates, of their own conceptual ignorance.

What Do Green Plants Need, Anyway?

A professor attached to a school of education at a major university teaches a graduate-level course for science majors who want to become school science teachers. Observe what happens when the professor brings a large mayonnaise jar into class, fills it halfway with dirt, plants a green plant, waters it, screws the lid on the jar, and asks the class, "What will happen to the plant?" Many students, especially the biology majors, call the experiment "murder" and predict that the plant will quickly die. Even the biology majors, it seems, still believe that plants and animals need the same living conditions—in this case, air.

Later, the alarmed professor brought the matter to the attention of members of the biology department, who were not particularly troubled by their graduates' ignorance. Said one, "I'm not surprised. We don't do botany any more. We're into molecular biology."

I asked a professor of biology at another university about this example. He explained it this way: "Molecular biology is an intensely competitive field. Professors must write proposals, obtain grants, conduct research, and keep up with a rapidly changing field. A professor's reputation as a scientist—his wealth and fame—depends upon his ability to keep up and publish in a very demanding area. If such a professor takes time out to review botany in order to teach it to undergraduates, his concentration on molecular biology is broken. He may miss a grant cycle."

A professor thus described is a caricature of professorial self-absorption, of careerism run amok. He appears to have little concern about whether the 15 percent or so of his students who are going to become biology teachers know and can teach about a basic life form, plants, and a basic branch of biology, botany. If the teachers are not prepared, though, it is not the biology department that is blamed, but the "methods courses," the "low standards for teacher education," and all the other usual suspects.

Simple Math Stumps Math Majors

A 1985 study by Alan Schoenfeld, a mathematician and math educator at the University of California at Berkeley, found that his undergraduates, most of whom had done well in college calculus as well as in high school geometry, had great difficulty explaining simple geometric problems.[5]

In 1988 Deborah Ball, an educational researcher at Michigan State University, found that math majors who planned to teach scored better than elementary education majors on dividing fractions, problems involving zero, and algebraic equations. But even the math majors had difficulty "making sense of division with fractions, connecting mathematics to the real world, and coming up with explanations that [went] beyond restatement of the rules."[6]

Borko and colleagues (1990) asked teacher candidates to generate a story problem based on the mathematical sentence, "1¾ divided by ½." A whopping 69 percent of the elementary education students were unable to do so. But a surprising 55 percent of the mathematics majors and minors who were planning to teach in secondary schools were also unable to devise a life situation that would call for that division problem. All could "work" the problem, of course, through the mechanical approach they had learned. But in trying to imagine a real-life situation using 1¾ divided by ½, many created a problem that involved dividing by 2 rather than by ½.[7] This study makes it clear that those math majors and minors didn't understand the *concept* of dividing by ½. If they had, they would have known that dividing by 2 produces a smaller number, whereas dividing by ½ produces a larger number. Engineers may not need to understand that concept, but teachers do.

Ball reports one student's fear that pupils would ask him a question like "Why are there negative numbers?"[8] It seems that those who cannot explain a concept do not fully understand it themselves.

The One True History

Like their counterparts in other academic disciplines, history professors claim the right, even when teaching undergraduates, to "profess" whatever positions their long years of study have led them to, or even to suppress divergent ideas, and undergraduate students of history are thereby denied access to lively and illuminating discussions and differences of opinion about the past. Even worse, they are too often subjected to the eminently forgettable routine of lectures and textbooks. To be sure, many professors of history do expose students to clashing perspectives, to original sources, and to historiography, but too many future teachers experience history in college as a laborious process of acquiring the "true facts" of a "true" story. That being the case, it is not surprising that many adult Americans, including teachers, hated history in school and college and now remember little of it, nor should we be surprised that teachers serving on a 1992 textbook adoption committee in Texas didn't balk at (or perhaps did not even recognize as an error) a textbook's claim that the Korean war ended because Harry Truman dropped the bomb.

"Imagine the difference between prospective teachers who experience history as an argument about what happened in the past and why, and those who encounter history as what is represented in a textbook," says G. Williamson McDiarmid of Michigan State University.[9] But at present, there is no assurance that history professors will engage their students in this argument, or that they will let their students in on the big secret of how historians "do" history and what constitutes valid evidence in history. Therefore, there is no assurance that taking more history courses will produce teachers who can fix the dates of the Civil War or remember who fought whom during World War II or care a fig about history.

Missing Topics

Many subjects that teachers are expected to teach in public school aren't taught in college. Fractions are an interesting case in point. As we have just seen, mathematics majors are rarely exposed to fractions, at least not as students in the mathematics department, which assumes that they already "know" these elementary topics. But public school teachers find the teaching of fractions enormously complex and often unsuccessful. Although the research literature on the teaching of fractions is as intellectually demanding as anything else in higher education, math departments seem oblivious to it. I told a number of mathematics professors what prospective and practicing teachers told me: that "elementary math methods" was tougher than calculus. Most of them blinked in disbelief; their lack of curiosity about learning, and about the workings of students' minds, seemed monumental.

Topics such as statistics and probability are beneath the dignity of many mathematics professors, and yet they are increasingly necessary tools of analysis in industrial quality control. "America is not going to get a quality revolution until its managers and workers have some grasp of probability and statistics—the *lingua franca* of quality," says Michael Schrage, a columnist for the *Los*

Angeles Times.[10] Schrage says that "corporate statistical literacy is abysmally low. Even our much vaunted Baldrige Award winners have trouble interpreting the language of quality." Schrage also reports that Brian Joyner, a Wisconsin-based consultant who works with several *Fortune* 500 companies on quality control issues, spends most of his time on remedial statistical education. "It's just as bad in the executive suite as on the factory floor," says Joyner. Schrage also quotes Temple University mathematics professor John Paulos, author of *Innumeracy* and *Beyond Numeracy:* "There's a kind of mathematician's snobbery, for lack of a better term, for dealing with the mathematics of everyday life." At present, it is far more likely that math educators, not mathematicians, are teaching future teachers to fill this crucial social and economic need.

English majors study theories of literary criticism, but not grammar. Therefore, a pure English major, untainted by education courses, is unlikely to remember very much from her own study of grammar, let alone know how to teach it. English departments are also frequently lackadaisical about teaching writing to undergraduates, as we will see in Chapter Four. They are rarely in the business of teaching their majors how to teach writing to others, yet that is one of the principal demands made on teachers of all subjects in today's public schools.

There is a widespread belief that people who earn degrees in a subject before even thinking about becoming teachers know more about, or are more passionately interested in, a subject than those who intended to become teachers all along because they "love children." This belief is part of the rationale for "alternate route" programs. For all the reasons already mentioned, however, these subject matter majors, untainted by education courses, are unlikely to know the right *kind* of "more," or even the "right stuff," and even less likely to know how to convey it to students than those who meet formal requirements for licensure.

This is not to dismiss the legitimate criticism of silly courses that still exist in many schools of education. But education in an academic discipline is no education at all if the student is not put to the intellectual labor of representing the discipline in lucid explanations, apt metaphors, and enlightening graphics; connecting the facts of the discipline to its underlying principles and to other bodies of knowledge; and applying the discipline to situations in life. Not only does such an education fail to serve future teachers; it fails all other students as well.

There is compelling evidence that deep knowledge of and enthusiasm for subject matter does underlie great school teaching. At issue, though, is the assumption that advanced coursework provides deep knowledge. That assumption flies in the face of the direct experience of most Americans who have ever attended college, as well as the research already cited. Yet the mantra "more studying of *what* to teach and less time learning *how* to teach" is still being chanted. It would probably be echoed by those Harvard graduates who don't know the answers to elemental scientific questions and don't know that they don't know.

To "Understand" Science

Andy (Charles W.) Anderson is a professor of science education at Michigan State University (MSU). Along with his colleagues at MSU and at the University of Michigan, Anderson has probed deeply into what it means to "understand" science.

Anderson and Roth (1989) have studied MSU students who have taken one or more college-level biology courses. They found that many could not apply their knowledge to situations in nature, much less explain what they knew to others. "Many students 'learn' science by memorizing large amounts of information in simple, list-like forms. While the list-like structures are useful for some limited purposes (such as answering recall questions), they are of little use for the more complex functions of description, explanation, prediction, and control." [11]

Even those prospective teachers who do understand are apt to have their knowledge and skill nullified by the curricula, textbooks, and tests they will be compelled to use as teachers. The public school norms, like those in universities, are to pile on the facts and hope that somehow students will make the connections and perceive the applications on their own.

Anderson advocates "teaching for conceptual change." This means that students must learn to alter their (usually wrong) folk understanding of how nature works and accept the (often counterintuitive) understanding sanctioned by the scientific community. For that to happen, teachers must "deeply understand" science themselves, know how to make scientific content accessible to students, and at the same time keep faith with the canons of science. The choice here is not between old-fashioned teaching versus new-fangled teaching, but between teaching methods that work for only a small minority of students and those that work for most students.

Producing teachers who know that much may seem like an impossible dream, but the MSU researchers have discovered such teachers and explored how they came to know what they know. To hear the voice of such a teacher as Mrs. Copeland is to make this approach to teaching seem a possible dream. "I kept coming back to those three questions. . . . Why a person dies when their heart stops?. . . . Why do we eat?. . . . Why do we breathe?. . . . especially the first one because they would say 'so what?' And I keep after them until they could tell me 'so what.' But if I hadn't asked them that question, I think they would have just memorized . . . they would have been able to identify the right words in the right places on the test and not have understood a thing . . . not understood what this has to do with them or living things or life functions at all."[12]

Teachers who were not like Mrs. Copeland but were generally regarded as good science teachers were found to be missing one or more of the elements required for teaching students to understand. Ms. Mitchell, for example, had an understanding of the connections between scientific ideas and processes, but lacked knowledge of real-world phenomena. Therefore, her subject matter knowledge wasn't rich enough to help her students think about the concepts they were studying.

Mr. Barnes had a rich science background, much teaching experience, and an awareness of his students' misconceptions about science, but he did not know that his simply telling students the right scientific answers wasn't likely to dispel their misconceptions. Although his lectures were virtuoso performances and models of correct scientific knowledge, lots of his students didn't work past their misconceptions toward correct understanding. In his own mind, his teaching was aimed at understanding, but the tests he administered required students to memorize many unconnected details, which he regarded as "content," and were not designed to detect whether students could understand and apply what they had learned. Mr. Barnes had a theory about why some students failed to "get it": they weren't very "organized," which meant that they weren't good at "processing information." For these students, Mr. Barnes's goal was not to teach them science but to help them become "better learners."

Anderson and Roth begin an article with a typical classroom exchange:

Teacher: Do you understand?

Student: Yes.

The student is answering honestly, as best he understands what the teacher means by "understand." But the science that the student has experienced thus far in school leads him to believe that "understanding" means the "ability to reduce knowledge of a scientific topic to a list of facts that can be memorized."[13] Most teachers think so, too.

Mrs. Copeland has discovered on her own how to teach for understanding. But it is clear, as in the cases of Ms. Mitchell and Mr. Barnes, that the discovery doesn't always come naturally through experience. Moreover, the isolation of teachers from one another means that Mrs. Copeland doesn't have any opportunity to share what she has learned with Ms. Mitchell and Mr. Barnes.

What Teachers Need

The "deep knowledge" teachers most need is the ability to answer the "why" and "what for" questions that their students ask. They also need other teachers, at every level, who recognize and explicitly deal with the obstacles students face as they struggle to understand, articulate, integrate, and apply new knowledge. If professors do not raise or cannot answer such questions, then we must raise questions about the depth of professors' knowledge. Back to Silberman: "To be an educator is to understand something of how to make one's education effective in the real world. It means to know something of how to apply knowledge to the life one lives and the society in which one lives it—in a word, to know what is relevant, and how to make knowledge relevant, which is to say, effective."[14]

John Goodlad, one of the nation's premier educational researchers, has argued with eloquence that the proper education of teachers in the liberal arts and sciences should be at the heart of the mission of even the most vaunted research university. Until that is so, our schools and society are in trouble.[15]

Many solutions to this problem have been tried and have failed. There are only two plausible ones that I can see: a patient, long-term hammering away at academics until they see what's in it for them to care about the next generation; or a more radical solution, seldom discussed in polite society, get rid of the tenure system and all the decay and distortions that it drags in its wake.

The six case studies that follow show how some better-than-average schools of education are coping with mounting pressure to improve the intellectual quality and teaching skill of the people who will teach the next generation of American children. The names of individuals have been changed, but the stories are all true.

Part One

New Ideas
in Teacher Education

2

Preparing Students for
the Real World of Teaching

An idyllic, expensive, liberal arts college with Ivy League
standards is turning out articulate, confident teachers who
are well prepared to teach the city's mostly poor, mostly
Hispanic public school students.

Trinity University sits astride a high ridge overlooking the city of
San Antonio. Groves of live oaks surround the university's salmon-
colored buildings, which are a harmonious mix of architectural
styles. Academically, Trinity is a top-ranked university. It is also
host to two professional schools, one for business and the other for
education.

   Trinity's department of education was celebrated on the front
page of the December 5, 1991, *Wall Street Journal* as an example
of a small trend toward excellence in teacher education.[1] The story
cites Susan Asprodites, who graduated from Trinity as a Phi Beta
Kappa and is now teaching third grade in San Antonio, as an example of the growing number of smart students entering the teaching profession.

   Asprodites and nine other academically able students were
lured to Trinity with a promise of scholarships, forgivable loans,

19

and $2,000 per year during the first two years of teaching. This package of enticements was assembled by Mark Jackson, chairman of Trinity's department of education, who was out to prove that highly able students could be recruited into teaching. The fact that several Trinity education students turn up on the Phi Beta Kappa list each year is a further enticement to students on and off campus who would like to become teachers if they can study in the company of intellectually stimulating classmates. The news story about Trinity emphasized that Asprodites "focused on English and history *instead of* education courses, and learned much of her technique from veteran teachers, *not* education professors" (emphasis mine; by italics, I am alerting the reader to an instance of the "either/or" assumption that has plagued the debate on teacher education for decades, and which made the newspaper story only half right, since teacher education at Trinity operates on a "both/and" assumption, a fusion of knowledge rather than a dichotomy, and a blending of the talents of academic professors, education professors, public school teachers, and students in training to be teachers).

Mark Jackson is widely acclaimed as the driving force behind a constellation of reform measures in Trinity's education program, officially launched in 1986. Trinity established alliances with four San Antonio schools where its interns teach and where its clinical faculty members work with principals and teachers, Trinity students, and school children. The college-school partnerships have already met the acid test: students in the allied schools have already demonstrated improvements in both achievement and attendance.[2] Jackson is a lanky, plainspoken man with a soft drawl and a gift for putting supplicants and visitors at ease. Everything he does seems unhurried and effortless. The tone of the department reflects Jackson's level personality and respectful attitude toward others.

Envious outsiders might suggest that the success of Trinity's education program rests on the cushion of its natural advantages. Trinity has high admission standards (an average SAT score of 1200), and no exceptions are made for those who want to become teachers. It is also an expensive school, with an annual tuition of $17,000. That fact alone tends to attract students whose privileged backgrounds enable them to do well in Trinity's rigorous liberal arts curriculum and to give all their time to their studies. Trinity also has the blessing of its small size: there are only 2,400 students on campus, and only 200 are in the department of education. Moreover, Mark Jackson's reform program did not begin at zero. Over many years, through various outreach programs, Trinity's education department had established a measure of mutual trust and respect with school leaders in the San Antonio area. Nevertheless, Jackson has brought an array of reforms into being that most other colleges, even those with similarly high standards, have only begun to attempt. Trinity abolished the undergraduate degree in elementary education in 1986. In its place, a new five-year program was created, composed of a four-year B.A. degree program in the humanities in education, and a fifth-year internship leading to an M.A. in teaching. As is true everywhere else, prospective secondary school teachers at Trinity major in the subjects they plan to teach.

The university's existing relationship with the four cooperating institutions—two elementary schools, one middle school, and one high school—was formalized in 1986 as the Alliance for Better Schools. Trinity students get out into the schools early. Freshmen and sophomores observe and tutor in the schools as part of their required work. Fifth-year interns spend an entire academic year under the supervision of outstanding teachers in the four schools. These teacher-mentors are also brought on campus to play a more formal role in teacher education.

To compensate the allied schools for the work they do on behalf of undergraduates and interns, Trinity's clinical professors work an amazing two or three days per week in those schools. They not only supervise the interns but also cover classes, collaborate with the teachers, and work on ways to bring more resources into the schools.

The program's design encourages esprit de corps among its students and graduates who are teaching locally (called "cohort groups" in the reform lingo), in the belief that teachers' isolation from one another not only has blocked the dissemination of knowledge about teaching but also has inhibited teachers from acting collectively on behalf of students. Trinity is also host to a variety of intellectual and cultural exchanges among the area's school superintendents and principals.

Few other universities in the United States have reported the achievement of, or even significant progress toward, this entire array of reforms. In a 1988 survey of the progress of schools of education toward reforms recommended by a variety of national reports, the American Association of Colleges of Teacher Education found that only 49 percent had mobilized incentives to attract good applicants, only 51 percent were using teachers to teach students, only 52 percent had increased liberal arts requirements, and only 5 percent had shifted to five-year programs. [3]

Trinity's B.A. degree in humanities in education, which has replaced the elementary education degree, is tailored to the knowledge needs of elementary teachers. "I rounded up some liberal arts faculty and ten master teachers, and they spent a year developing the program," Jackson says casually, as if it had been a lark to persuade research-minded professors to spend their time visiting elementary schools and seeking advice from teachers on the design of academic courses. Elsewhere—indeed, nearly everywhere—such attempts have been thwarted by arts and science faculties.

Hispanic Children and Anglo-American Teachers

San Antonio's population is now 60 percent Hispanic, and the students in Trinity's teacher education program are overwhelmingly Anglo. I asked one Trinity student where she was learning about the culture of the students she would be teaching. Her answer, more than any list of course titles, captures the flavor of Trinity's humanities in education program: "I learned a lot about the history and culture of San Antonio in a course on cities. In an art class, we studied the architecture here by visiting the missions and cathedrals, and our history course included Latin American history. In a strand on religion, I studied the Catholic and Pentecostal churches, which was good because I didn't know anything about either one."

Still, there are problems at Trinity with the kinds of content taught by arts and science faculty. The mathematics department does not offer geometry, for example, because it is not considered college-level mathematics. That is a problem for graduates who go out to teach it, with only the distant memory of the subject from their high school years. The National Council for Accreditation of Teacher Education (NCATE) may offer the teacher educators at

Trinity some useful leverage with the math department, since NCATE's report on its most recent inspection of the Trinity teacher education program did note the absence of geometry courses. NCATE currently lacks the power to enforce its standards, which are becoming more rigorous, but its imprimatur is nevertheless valuable to Trinity.

Fundamental concepts and connections in the academic disciplines are also sometimes missing from Trinity's undergraduate courses. A member of the education faculty observed, "The big push for more courses in the arts and sciences derived from the observation that many high school teachers didn't know their subjects deeply enough and couldn't help their students make the important connections. But many highly educated people, including college professors, don't know how all the bits and pieces of their disciplines fit together, or if they do, they've had no practice in explaining it to someone else. Taking more courses in a discipline won't solve the problem. The issue is the nature of university teaching, as well as whether college professors are willing to teach basic topics in their fields, topics that are not currently fashionable research areas."

Some of the arts and sciences faculty members I interviewed did understand the problem. Barry Minton, a biology professor, has won three awards for his teaching. He is aware of the research on the pedagogy of content and on misconceptions that students bring to the science classroom. He has been active in the movement to reform precollege science education and has made a study of college-level biology textbooks. He would like to do research on how to make learning more efficient. But, he says, "My administrative superiors tell me I'm wasting my time: 'Educational pedagogy is not science.' Bench [disciplinary] science, no matter what an institution professes to the contrary, is the best value. The way to get salary raises is to get grants to do scientific research and to publish."

Sidney Williston, president of Trinity University, told me that since Trinity is primarily a liberal arts school, "the real and first issue is teaching—an indifferent teacher will not be maintained." At the same time, he acknowledged the resistance of academics to cooperating with education faculty: "If you put a math educator in a pure math department, the contempt is enormous."

Nevertheless, Williston still insists (although softly) that even the clinical faculty in the education program must meet the publication standards required of pure academics. Yet, as we saw in Chapter One, researchers around the nation, some of them bona fide mathematicians, are discovering that mathematics majors taught by pure mathematicians are conceptually weak and often unable to answer students' questions. A teacher who merely knows how to do math may not know enough to teach it well.

Bridging the chasm between content and pedagogy is a challenge to teacher educators in every state. The State of Texas has compounded the problem. State law now limits to eighteen credit hours the number of education courses that can be required. Therefore, education departments all over the state have few credit hours in which to fill gaps in students' content knowledge or teach them how to make use of the relevant research base in pedagogical content knowledge.

The compensating strength of the Trinity program is the fifth-year internship, which gives students a full year of protected practice under the guidance of teacher-mentors whom the university has had a hand in choosing. Because interns assume the full burden of teaching, grading, and paperwork only gradually, they can take time to listen to and get to know the students. They can try out, a little at a time, what they have learned through study and observation. When things go badly, the mentor is there to pick up the pieces. In evening pedagogy seminars, interns analyze and critique one another's triumphs and disasters.

The Trinity faculty and mentors have worked hard to teach interns the skills of classroom management, and the fruits of their labor are easy to observe. I witnessed a scene at Jackson-Keller Elementary School, where a second-grade class taught by a Trinity-trained teacher was about to go off to lunch. "Where's my line leader?" the teacher asked. A boy leapt up and, in a matter of seconds, was standing smartly at the door. As in a choreographed ballet, the rest of the class composed itself into an orderly line behind the leader—no bumping or shoving. In unison, the children patted themselves on the back and marched off jauntily to the cafeteria, plainly delighted with themselves, and their teacher was delighted with them. Carol Todorovic, the Trinity professor assigned to Jackson-Keller, says that smooth transitions like the one I watched save a lot of instructional time, as well as wear and tear on teachers. She challenges interns to invent repertoires of transition routines that meet her criteria: "They must be rhythmic, the students should enjoy them, and they should not become boring from overuse."

Interns must also learn to squelch their natural impulses in certain situations. A mentor told me about Jimmy, a new boy at school who was upset because his father was in jail: "The intern was in charge of the class when Jimmy had a tantrum. When I came back, Jimmy was in the corner, and the rest of the class was quiet. The intern was bug-eyed, worried about whether she had handled the tantrum correctly. She had. In her pedagogy seminar, she had been taught to walk away and let the child cool off, and she was able to resist the natural instinct to scream at the child."

Trinity's program is built around the theme of the "reflective practitioner." Teachers are encouraged to examine their own teaching critically and continually. I saw evidence that the practice of self-examination had become habitual. One teacher, for example, talked about the advantages of the daily alternation between teaching and reflecting on teaching: "I like being at Mark Twain every day and at Trinity in class every night. I wrote my seminar papers on metaphors, nonverbal communication, the philosophy of education, and politics and power. We talk about these things at night, and during the day we look for examples of how these broad ideas play out in class. I've learned that some metaphors confuse students or carry underlying meanings I didn't intend. Other metaphors help students claim ownership of an idea."

Interns and first-year teachers praised the education and training they had received at Trinity, although most also said they could have used more instruction in methods and techniques. This response varies sharply from the national data on teachers' assessments of their training. Those data show that teachers tend to think of such courses as a waste of time. The discrepancy may have several explanations. Trinity's courses are less theoretical than practical. Trinity students get to try out methods with children while they are learning them in class, and so their courses seem more meaningful to them. Students from traditional programs are so overwhelmed by classroom-discipline problems in the first year that they forget what they have learned, even if it was well taught and useful. Criticism from elites of methods courses exerts a not-so-subtle pressure on most teachers to disparage their own education courses or else be considered stupid. And most methods courses really *are* awful, and that is why teachers say so in surveys.

Trinity's interns and recent graduates did not praise the Texas state department of education or have many kind things to say about the effects of its regulations on teachers and schools. Complaints about the state's third-grade reading test were numerous, but this one stood out: "The test is a typographical nightmare. Even an adult would have trouble reading it! The 'bubbles' the kids are supposed to darken are embedded in the text, but in the wrong places. The questions are phrased in such an awkward way that even children who know the answer perfectly well don't realize what the question is. And there are grammatical errors in the test."

"It's unprofessional to give a child an ungrammatical test," I replied. "Have you thought about writing a letter to the state commissioner, or an article for the newspaper?"

"I couldn't," she said. "I would have to use examples to make the point, and that would be a violation of test security. People have been fired for that in this state."

Teachers' reluctance to complain publicly may be explained by the fact that those I interviewed did not yet have the security of tenure. But even a school principal, who also had complained about the test, retreated into submissiveness when I pushed her: "We have to be responsive to what the public values, and the public values these tests."

Would the public, especially its educated members, still value these tests if they had an opportunity to read them? Probably not, but the dire threats aimed at would-be violators of "test security" will probably continue to discourage whistle-blowers.

There were also complaints about the state's teacher evaluation system, a complicated checklist, divorced from subject matter, that pits teachers against one another. One beginner said, "I was going to teach a lesson on clouds, and I asked an experienced teacher if she could give me some ideas. She told me that her lesson on clouds was the one she was going to use when the evaluator came around, and she had no intention of sharing it, because she wanted to get points for originality."

Trinity's education faculty feels cramped by the state's regulatory excesses. Teachers in the state are judged according to the "lesson cycle" of Madeline Hunter,[4] and so Trinity faculty feel obliged to prepare students to teach in that manner. At the same time, however, education students are given to understand that the "frontal teaching" required by the Hunter method does not advance students' understanding of many topics or their mastery of certain skills and so should be used sparingly. Students are taught to use many methods, but they are also taught the advantages and disadvantages of them all.

The Trinity teachers and mentors I watched in action worked at a level far higher than the highest level required by the state's accountability system, and so did many of their students. At Hawthorne Elementary School, for example, I read clear and correct compositions by very young children. The kids' scores in writing had soared, but the state's standardized tests were not designed to capture the advances in reading and thinking that frequent writing produces. Faculty members were frustrated on that account.

A paper written by a second grader on the occasion of Martin Luther King's birthday—the assignment was "tell your own dream"—was not only good but also moving: "I dream that there will be no gangs. I dream that I will not be made to join a gang when I get older. I dream that my brother can leave the gang and not get hurt." Gangs proliferate in the poor, transient, mainly Hispanic neighborhood around Hawthorne. The power of the Trinity-Hawthorne alliance to mitigate those circumstances can be seen in the school's relationship to its community. The faculty called a meeting of parents and asked them to stay in the school's attendance zone so that their children would have some stability in their lives—friends and neighbors rather than gangs. School officials promised to help families find housing or rent money. The strategy worked: only a few families moved out of the school's zone last year.

Trinity wants its students to speak up and take responsibility for shaping education policy and professional practice. Perhaps because of the school's philosophy, its students were the most assertive and least passive I saw anywhere. Their comparative assertiveness may also reflect the fact that most of them come from white, upper-middle-class families, with all the self-confidence that majority status, community standing, and financial stability can bestow.

Nevertheless, there was a noticeable difference between the students' assertiveness in campus classes and their more muted behavior as first-year teachers. When these beautifully trained students leave the hothouse of Trinity's atmosphere and enter the arid, regulated environment of the state's public schools, they seem to wilt—initially, at least. The social and economic problems that are overwhelming San Antonio's children also take their toll on these bright young teachers.

Is there a mismatch between the affluent white Trinity students and the mostly minority students in the allied schools? Some interns and beginning teachers said that they were deeply pained by the chaos in their students' lives. Others resented the fact that teachers were being held responsible for the learning of children who were sick, hungry, or distraught because of family problems. Nevertheless, the Trinity graduates seemed resolute in their expectation that the children would become readers, writers, problem solvers, and high school graduates. The topic of self-esteem came up in their conversations, but not in a way that smacked of disabling condescension or low expectations. Some of the Trinity students I interviewed had taken the trouble to learn Spanish. Nearly all their Hispanic students spoke English, but these teachers found that a little Spanish here and there helped establish trust.

Trinity's education department has made maximum use of its natural advantages to achieve a very high standard in teacher education. But there are natural disadvantages, too. In this university that sees itself as an elite institution, where "real" academics do research, teacher educators have the uncommonly difficult task of persuading arts and sciences faculty to change what they teach and how they teach it. If they cannot influence the way in which academic courses are taught, then they are severely constrained from taking matters into their own hands: recall the state legislature's limit on the number of education courses that can be required. Nevertheless, Mark Jackson and his colleagues, along with the principals and teachers in the allied schools and a highly intelligent cadre of students, have created effects greater than the sum of the program's parts.

3

Can the Disciplines
Work Together?

The University of Texas at San Antonio's Interdisciplinary
Studies Program for future elementary school teachers is
a shining example of what can happen when academic
faculties and teacher educators cooperate around the goal
of a broad, integrated, challenging liberal arts program for
those who will be teaching all subjects.

In 1972 the University of Texas at San Antonio (UTSA) was established on the western outskirts of San Antonio. All the buildings on
campus are bland, bulky structures that seem to have been built
around the same time. Yet their setting—rolling hills, with clumps
of live oak trees and clumps of cactus—eases the impression of
starkness.

UTSA's mission, I was told, is to provide a relatively low-cost
higher education to San Antonio's less-than-affluent and mainly Hispanic population. Unfortunately, the site is many miles away from
most of the low-income students it was established to serve. Students
must either drive or spend hours commuting by bus. Perhaps as a
consequence, the percentage of Hispanic students enrolled (40 percent) is disproportionately lower than the Hispanic population of

the city. Even so, the school of education is qualifying a substantial number of Hispanics for membership in a profession that sorely needs them.

Most of UTSA's education students are earning their way through school, taking care of families, or both. They must juggle course offerings with all the other demands on their time. There are some upper-middle-class students and military retirees, a number of women who commute from the small towns outside San Antonio, and city people who feel unstable in their current occupations. Most students earn their degrees a little at a time, and the university offers classes well into the evening hours to accommodate its students' complicated lives.

The Interdisciplinary Studies (IDS) Program

The most remarkable aspect of UTSA's teacher education program is its liberal arts curriculum for future elementary school teachers. When the state legislature mandated an undergraduate degree in an academic subject (Texas still permits undergraduate degrees in early childhood education, reading, bilingual education, and special education) and imposed an eighteen-credit-hour ceiling on education courses, UTSA responded to that new law creatively.

The education faculty saw no virtue in requiring the future elementary school teachers to major in just one subject, when they would be expected to teach all of them, and so they created the Interdisciplinary Studies Program, in 1989. The development of the program required acrobatic leaps across disciplinary boundaries. One "strand," for example, is the course "Science and Humanity," developed with the collaboration of scholars in biology, chemistry, physics, philosophy, religion, and art.

In moving to a required sequence of interdisciplinary courses for all elementary education students, UTSA, like Trinity, took advantage of its natural assets. The university is young, and its faculty are new, flexible, and service-minded. Enough professors believed in the concept that its development was accomplished by committed volunteers, not reluctant draftees. For example, Malcolm Grier, a professor of history and an IDS faculty member, conducts research in his field, modern European history, and publishes regularly. He has no graduate assistant, and even if there were a budget for one, he would have a hard time finding one with the skill he requires—fluency in German. Besides keeping up his scholarship, he has been one of the principal organizers of the Interdisciplinary Studies Program and teaches two of its courses, "World Civilization to the Fifteenth Century" and "World Civilization Since the Fifteenth Century." Most of the students in his classes are future elementary school teachers, but there are some history majors as well.

Grier is a believer in interdisciplinary education. "IDS courses were designed to give more coherence to the core undergraduate education program," he says. He is also not one to look askance at teacher education: "Some of us have deliberately formed links between the disciplines and education. There was initial resistance from teacher education students who didn't want to take the course, because the demands on students are greater than in the survey course in U.S. history." He says that his students have difficulty with writing, but he still requires three essay exams each semester: "People actually learn if they are given a fair amount of direction and advice on how to write an essay." He grades hundreds of essays each semester, and he is apologetic about not having the time to mark them up with as much care as he would wish.

In the eyes of an academic like Malcolm Grier, disciplinary scholarship, broad knowledge, teaching, and the teaching of teachers are a seamless web. Although his pride in his scholarly achievements is evident, he takes no pleasure in setting himself above others on that account. Not only does he appreciate the connections between good university teaching and good school teaching, he has gone out of his way to forge such connections.

I watched Professor Anna Sauvage teach "Modes of Inquiry Across the Fields of Study" in a classroom of some forty students, most of them older than traditional undergraduates. The class was exploring what could be learned about a historical time and place through the study of artifacts. The text—one of a great many books that the students were expected to read in the course—had been written by Sauvage herself, about nineteenth-century life in a nearby town. The students had been assigned to write essays about any one of four artifacts that Sauvage explored in her book: a wedding portrait, a wish list, a Watkins bottle, and a house plan.

Sauvage divided the class into four groups, according to the artifacts that they had chosen to write about.

I sat in on the Watkins-bottle group, where the discussion revolved around forms of evidence. The students in the group stayed on task and seemed interested in the topic, but the pressures that made their lives so different from those of Trinity's students sometimes erupted into the discussion—broken cars, unreliable babysitters, not enough time to get to the library.

Later, the whole class discussed the house plan, a drawing of the room arrangements in a nineteenth-century farmhouse, as well as a photograph of the house.

"I think it's crazy to have the kitchen on one end of the house and the living room on the other," said one male student. "You'd have to go through the children's bedrooms to take food or drinks to the living room."

"That was for fire protection," said a female student. "See how the kitchen has stone walls around it? And there is a breezeway between the kitchen and the rest of the house. That was to protect the rest of the house in case of a kitchen fire."

"Besides," added a woman in her forties, "they didn't do hors d'œuvres and cocktails in those days, so there wasn't any reason to take food from the kitchen to the living room."

"But there isn't even a door to the outside from the living room," said the first student, evidently irked by the house design.

"It isn't really a living room, it's a parlor," said a middle-aged woman. "And people used it for special guests, and just for talking. Not having a door to the outside was a way of keeping the dust off the good furniture and draperies."

"Why would they have a door from the master bedroom to the outdoors? Isn't that dangerous?" asked a young woman. She had the look of someone who lived in a condo with an electronic security system.

"They didn't have to worry about security back then," answered another student.

"Why do you suppose they had a swept lawn?" asked Sauvage, referring to the photograph that showed a border of bare earth around the house, neatly swept, with plants and flowers commencing at a distance of five or so feet.

"Fire protection," someone offered.

And so it went, in a lively, free-flowing interchange between the yuppies and the middle-aged, between those who were enmeshed in the assumptions of their own time and place and those who were not, between those who immediately saw something alien as stupid and those who tried to figure out why things might have been done differently. The ostensible purpose may have been to teach students the process of inquiry in history—how judgments are made and facts are established. But a secondary purpose, confirmed by Professor Bertrand Metts, who also teaches the course, seemed to be to induce an anthropological pause, a catching of the breath in the presence of the unfamiliar and inexplicable—a useful habit of mind for teachers, especially those who teach children from many cultures and traditions.

Sauvage was as good a teacher as I had ever seen on a college campus. The kinds of epistemological questions that were discussed in her course are the very kinds that teachers need most and that most academics avoid, at least with undergraduates. If the best way to break the pattern of bad teaching is for future teachers to see good teaching, then Anna Sauvage was doing a masterful job of demonstrating another vision of what it means to teach. Even in an overlarge class with students of quite varying abilities, she seemed to know not only who everyone was but where everyone was intellectually, and to respond to all the students with the lightness of a master and the ease of someone who trusts the native intelligence of her students.

Later, I found that I was not alone in my admiration for both the course and the teacher. "Modes of Inquiry," taught by several members of the IDS faculty, is the pride of the program and the gateway to teacher education.

Sauvage receives high ratings from her students for the quality of her teaching. She explained to me her goals for students in her course: "One of the most important things for teachers to develop is the motivation to investigate, the propensity to ask oneself whether one really understands, and the knowledge of where to find information."

Edgar Kilbane, a professor of political science, teaches another portion of the IDS sequence, a three-hour course called

"Individual, Family, Community." In it he tries to induct students into a scientific way of thinking about social issues, choosing the most highly charged themes—power, class, gender, ethnicity, and race—as vehicles for organizing students' investigations into what social scientists do and what theories they use. I asked what kinds of works the students were reading—*Habits of the Heart,* perhaps?

"Too preachy," Kilbane said. "The first year of the course, I tried using Marx, Weber, and Freud, but it didn't work. Now I try to present them with a lot of data."

Kilbane finds his students resistant to social science, especially "women from the country" who have very conventional views and plan to teach in their home communities. He portrays them as "extremely relativistic"; confronted with data that could disturb their opinions, they say, "It's only your opinion." When I suggested that the social sciences were not neutral, that there are inherent value positions even in statistics, he seemed unimpressed.

Kilbane also observes that "women from the country" have such a deep belief in individual freedom and responsibility that they resist notions of social responsibility. I did not get to watch Kilbane's class, but my sense was of a clash between cultures: the "women from the country," probably middle-aged, Protestant, Republican, and prideful of their faithfulness and respectability, and the professor, young, probably secular and politically liberal, and prideful of his rationality. The class, as described by Kilbane, sounded like a replay of modern school wars: on one side, educators who believe that they are presenting hard evidence winnowed from technically correct and scientific procedures, and who are annoyed when amateurs with raw opinions put up resistance; and, on the other, parents who believe, without being able to explain why, that there are alien values hidden in the data, and who resent the educator's pose of scientific neutrality.

In marked contrast to the scientism of Kilbane's course, the IDS course that explores the hard sciences also unabashedly treats religion and ethics. Glen Hofheinz, a professor of philosophy, not only teaches the course but also wrote the textbook. If his students learn what he intends them to learn, then this course is a remarkably powerful contribution to their knowledge about knowledge. Hofheinz explores the kinds of judgments that scientists can make, and he helps students explore the boundary between scientific knowledge and dialectical knowledge. Teachers who recognize the point at which science can no longer stake its claim—where human value judgments and the skills of dialectical argument must take the discussion toward an ethical, religious, or political conclusion—are worth their weight in gold.

Methods and Foundations at UTSA

The energy and talent that brought about the IDS undergraduate sequence for future teachers apparently ran out of steam before it reached UTSA's school of education itself. There were bright spots and smart people, but there were also courses that confirmed some of the worst stereotypes. The courses I observed might have been better on other days. While I was there, however, the professors seemed to be indoctrinating the students into the formula teaching required by the state's teacher evaluation system and official curriculum guide. I saw no evidence that these future teachers were being exposed to any warnings about limitations or pitfalls of these approaches. Perhaps because so little time is allowed for teaching the many things that teachers need to know, the methods courses seemed to be covering too much ground, and covering it trivially.

Some of the same students I had observed acting like intelligent adults in the IDS classes were acting like klutzy kids here. ("Forgot to look at the questions." "Brought the wrong notebook.")

It didn't get any better in a class on philosophy of education. Sitting in the back of the room, I saw winces and grins on the faces of Hispanic students as the professor laboriously called the roll, mispronouncing a fair number of names. He gave a lecture on the educational philosopher George Herbert Mead, drawn from the text of a journal reprint from 1980. It might have been a perfectly fine lecture for people who had spent many years laboring in the schools and were now prepared to ponder, at the Ph.D. level, the large ideas in education. But the lecture and text were light years away from these students, not only because they lacked the basis in experience to appreciate them but also because they did not know the language peculiar to academic educationists: "Mead sets forth a 'psychological statement of the act,' which is a heuristic device by which he investigates a multitude of facets involved in the enterprise of education."

On the bright side, and reflecting the pragmatism that characterizes teacher education at its best, Burton Thorman, a professor of reading at UTSA, is fighting a lonely stop-gap action against the excesses of the national cult that has sprung up around the "whole language" movement. Thorman supports most of the tenets of the movement. He thinks that kids should get to read really good books from the start, rather than being drilled on meaningless exercises. Nevertheless, he sees the importance of also integrating decoding into reading instruction right from the start, an idea that raises hackles in the extremist wing of the movement. Just as traditional teachers have killed children's interest in reading by surrendering their jobs to the teacher manuals, Thorman now sees too many "whole language" teachers surrendering their job to a romantic ideology: "In the more ideological approaches, kids learn only one strategy, and when that doesn't work, they are lost." The kids who come to school with little home support, says Thorman, "need more explicit teaching" than they are getting from the fanatic partisans of "whole language."

The legislative cap on methods courses in this state, according to Thorman, has compromised the all-important effort of preparing elementary school teachers to teach reading. He believes that learning how to teach reading—how to detect the ways each child learns best—is a complicated matter and can be accomplished only with close supervision of novice teachers in the classroom.

"Before the legislation," Thorman says, "we used to have a six-hour reading practicum with students out in the field. We could critique what the teacher did and talk with her about it. But after the legislation, that was seen as 'pedagogy,' and reading got bumped into the generic supervision of elementary education."

Thorman is not the only professor frustrated by the limitations imposed by the state legislature. Meryle Bates, a professor of elementary education, has worked with both traditionally trained and "alternate route" teachers and spoke about the consequences of insufficient pedagogical training: "Untrained teachers don't understand developmental levels. A student who hasn't had a lot of experience with textbooks, or who doesn't know what a child of a given age can do, has no idea what students can read, write, or accomplish in half an hour." Without a deep understanding of Piagetian stages, says Bates, teachers confuse students by giving them work that is too abstract.

Student Teaching at UTSA

UTSA chose not to have a fifth-year program, "because of competition from other, nearby colleges which were not going that way," says Frank Morse, coordinator of student teaching at UTSA. Therefore, UTSA must provide prospective teachers with classroom experience in the old-fashioned way, by devoting the last half of the senior year to student teaching. (This decision is an example of how market competition can lower rather than raise standards.) As in most other large schools of education (UTSA has about three hundred student teachers every semester), providing future teachers with field experience is a cumbersome matter, now made more cumbersome by state legislation requiring pre-student teaching experiences—one of the better features of the new law.

To improve the quality of field experiences, UTSA has established a collaborative arrangement with two elementary schools in the San Antonio Independent School District and two more in the nearby Edgewood Independent School District. These schools, says Morse, provide a concentrated venue for students' field experience. Pre-student teachers now spend two hours a week observing in these schools while they are taking their elementary methods course.

Student teachers have little supervisory contact with senior faculty members like Morse; the sheer number of student teachers makes such contact nearly impossible. Instead, as in most large schools, student teachers are monitored by low-paid student teacher supervisors, teachers with master's degrees and at least three years of teaching experience. They are regarded as part-time faculty and are "paid miserably," says Morse. "But they enjoy the influence they can have, and many like the job because, for one reason or another, they want part-time work." Each supervisor carries twenty-four students and visits them four times during the semester—a far cry from the intensive faculty involvement with Trinity interns. UTSA provides minimal training to the cooperating teachers, who are volunteers.

Out in the Schools

Joe, a first-year high school math teacher who graduated from UTSA, had few criticisms of his college training but many about the insanities of the system: "I had some good professors, and the only criticism I have is that you don't get any direct experience with kids before student teaching. Videotapes of teaching, or even teaching before your peers, would help, but direct experience with students would be preferable."

Another of Joe's criticisms was that UTSA's exit test in mathematics was "too low." The test, pegged to the state curriculum, "is based on upper-track high school mathematics." Joe believes that a high school mathematics teacher ought to know mathematics far beyond the content taught to high school students.

Joe put his finger on an endemic problem in American education: student teachers are usually assigned to experienced teachers who have the seniority to cadge the advanced classes, but first-year teachers are assigned to low-track classes and therefore have no previous exposure either to the kinds of kids they will teach in those classes or the topics they will study. For example, Joe is teaching pre-algebra and geometry; another first-year teacher in his school "has five low-level classes and spends most of her time on discipline and special education."

Even in his weak position as a first-year teacher, however, Joe stood up to the fury of the coach and the parents when he gave a failing grade to the star football player. In doing so, he was implementing the state's "no pass, no play" law. "There were anonymous letters and threatening phone calls," Joe said, "but I carefully checked the rules and regulations and made sure I had the principal's support. The student knew he earned the failing grade and accepted responsibility for it. This semester he earned a B." Joe said, with the smile of satisfaction one sees in teachers who love their work.

Mimi, another first-year teacher, worked in business before going into teaching. At twenty-eight, she is now teaching physical education in a middle school. "I use a lot of procedures I learned at UTSA—lesson plans, schedules, and organizing. I learned a lot about testing and measurement from a class at UTSA taught by a school administrator." She is skeptical about "the lesson cycle," by which she means the state's approved generic teaching method. "We don't know how to put content in that, and there wasn't very much content-specific training in the program."

The New Director of Teacher Education

Alexander Dietz has just come to UTSA to head up the department of education. As a newcomer, he is free to look at the program with some detachment; as someone responsible for setting new directions, he is thinking about the big picture. "The Interdisciplinary Studies Program is a good effort," he says, "but we need faculty working in the schools—joint appointments in education and the disciplines." The obstacle, according to Dietz, is not so much convincing the administrators to be more flexible as convincing the arts and science faculty: even if they say yes, they retreat when they are facing tenure and review.

Dietz seems pleased with the supervision of student teaching, but he is concerned about the selection of supervising teachers. "We need more power in selecting cooperating teachers, and we are beginning to negotiate that with the school districts and principals."

He worries about another state mandate, to provide induction programs for first-year teachers—certainly a fine idea, but "there is no funding for the universities or the school districts." In a classic case of mandate-without-money, the state has told the school districts to get on with induction programs anyway, and Dietz would like to help, but the university has no money either.

I asked Dietz why the campus classes were so overcrowded. "I can't just go out and hire people," he said. "The state funding formula for positions is two years out of phase, and we have to wait until this legislature adjusts the formula." He is planning to set enrollment limits that are based on the number of placements available for student teaching.

I also asked Dietz about the prospects for teaching becoming a true profession.

"NCATE hasn't done it," he said, "and the National Board for Professional Teaching Standards, or one of those efforts, has got to deliver."

Moving the Right Way

UTSA's teacher education program has done heroic work in planning and executing a thoughtful academic program of studies for its undergraduates who plan to teach in elementary schools. UTSA also seems willing to educate, rather than weed out, the many students who come to its program lacking college-level skills and a middle-class orientation. In this respect, UTSA is playing the historic role of teacher colleges—to take those who are the first members of their families to go to college and give them a boost up the ladder of opportunity. Academic expectations for these students seem fairly high. The students themselves are earnest and grateful for the chance to become professionals, and there is no reason to doubt that many among them will become those "brightest and best" that the reform reports call for.

At the same time, the teacher training program itself seems spotty and has been hampered by the state legislature's political spasm over teacher education. If the legislature's motive was to get rid of vacuous methods courses, it may only have made the courses even more vacuous than before because they are now so compressed.

The teachers make it clear that subject matter education is not enough. There is a lot to know about teaching and learning, about planning a curriculum, about students' growth and development, about families and society, and about such pedestrian matters as getting kids from the classroom to the lunchroom without risking a riot. This knowledge does not come naturally to more than a handful of people; once teachers are locked into their individual classrooms, it may take them years to discover it through brute experience. The public and the politicians are not wrong to think that this knowledge has often been badly transmitted, but that is no argument for killing a necessary enterprise through successive amputations.

UTSA, like Trinity, labors under the burden of the state's excessively bureaucratic, frequently out-of-date, and sometimes wrongheaded regulatory and political apparatus. Nevertheless, UTSA has made an impressive start on the task of improving the academic education of teachers and is making the right moves to integrate subject matter, pedagogy, and experience.

4

Guarding the Gates
to the Profession

Maryville University education students get a balanced liberal arts education and a tough but nurturing teacher education aimed at producing teachers who are reflective
about their work. The nurturing environment is tempered,
however, by the faculty's determination to guard the gates
to the profession.

Maryville University was founded in 1872 by the Religious of the
Sacred Heart as an academy for young women. Although it has
since become a private, nonsectarian, coeducational university, the
campus reveals its history—a chapel at the center, and nondescript
classroom buildings and dormitories around a peaceful quadrangle.
The school's offerings reflect the values of the founders—service to
the community. One-fourth of the student body is enrolled in business or business-related programs, but there are still many students
preparing to become nurses, physical therapists, and teachers or to
work in other occupations concerned with improving the human
condition. Many of the course titles in the traditional academic
departments have a human-service tilt, and the university's goals for
students are unabashedly moral and ethical.

Tough Love

The most striking feature of Maryville's education program is the
intensity of the faculty's involvement with students. Faculty
members work a sixty-hour week, and some of those hours involve
evening telephone conversations with fledgling teachers who have
had a bad day in class. The nurturing atmosphere and ready avail-
ability of faculty members to student, however, is linked to high
academic standards. About 15 percent of the students wash out of
the program in the sophomore year, and another 5 percent leave at
the end of the junior year. Elizabeth Wren, chair of the division of
education, exemplifies the program's character—compassion, combined with toughness and openness to criticism.

The largely female faculty (eight women, four men), along
with the small size of the school, may explain the depth of the
personal and intellectual connections between faculty and students.
There are only 3,000 students on campus, with a total of only 350
students in the undergraduate and graduate teacher education programs. A large portion of the 3,000 students are enrolled in the week-
end college, however, and so the weekday atmosphere of the campus
is serene and intimate. Quite a few of the students in the preservice
education program are in their thirties and forties, having decided
to teach after raising their families, or after some years of experience
in other lines of work. Quite a few of the students in the postbaccalaureate program also did other kinds of work before deciding to
become teachers.

The motif of the program is "the teacher as a reflective practitioner." The education professors continually demonstrate this
habit of reflection and self-examination within easy hearing of their
students, who endlessly flow in and out of the division's cramped
office suite. A "reflection paper" is required of each student at the
end of each semester. The faculty use this device to chart students'
analytical and personal development.

Shock Treatment

Another striking feature of Maryville's program is its conscious
attempt to dispel students' myths about teaching. It is commonly

observed that laymen think teaching is easy—you just stand up there and tell people what they should know. Yet there comes the moment for teachers-in-training when this sort of confidence suddenly dissolves, and fear strikes. Often the moment comes too late—when the student has already invested three or more years of work and tuition into becoming a teacher and is therefore reluctant to back out.

Maryville aggressively acts on the assumption that its entering students do not yet understand what it means to be a teacher. It provokes an early crisis in self-confidence by sending its undergraduate students out to work in both urban and suburban schools in the sophomore year—the better to discourage those who are not cut out for teaching. Students spend three mornings a week at schools "where good things are going on," says Nicole Stewart, a professor in the department. Simultaneously, the students are enrolled in education courses, which help them critique and interpret what they are seeing and doing in the schools. Before formal student teaching begins, in the senior year, students will have spent three hundred to four hundred hours in classrooms.

I witnessed the kind of crisis in self-confidence that Maryville's early exposure program is designed to provoke. A smart young woman, seeking teaching credentials after earning a degree in history at a good state university, burst into the division's conference room, where several faculty members were explaining the program to me. Fresh from a bad experience, she had come to tell Elizabeth Wren about her new doubts. Her panic overwhelmed any reluctance she might have had about spilling out her fears before me, a total stranger, and her professors.

"Lecturing was how I was taught, not how I learn," she began, "and I don't really know *anything* about history." She was having a hard time writing objectives for a history lesson, because she felt that her content was weak. Moreover, she had no idea of how to engage her students with the content. Selecting the right material, deciding how to present it, and discovering what the students did and did not know suddenly seemed like insuperable obstacles. "I don't have a frame of reference for 'teaching models,'" she said. "Where do they come from, and how do I implement them? I'm scared, and I need to prove to myself that I can do it. But I can't grow past my maturity. I'm only twenty-two years old and still dependent on my parents."

She had already shared her panic with her parents, who had suggested that she was making a mountain out of a molehill. Wren echoed the same idea, but much more tactfully, and offered some anxiety-reducing advice: "Ask the teacher to team-teach the lesson, so all the burden doesn't fall on you. And do a lecture, if you need to, for the sake of your own comfort." After some conversation, the young woman left the room more relaxed than before. A question lingered in my mind: How had she earned a degree in history at a great state university without knowing *"anything* about" history?

An Intensive Student-Teaching Experience

Whether seniors are scheduled for student teaching in the fall or the spring semester, they all must show up for a "September experience" in the classes where their student teaching will occur. They learn what it means to unpack supplies, set up a classroom for the year, and plan a long sequence of lessons. When the children arrive, they learn how a teacher sets the tone and establishes the rules, and how she gets the kids in harness for a year's work.

Student teachers take responsibility for a sequence of learning, not just for isolated lessons. They spend two seven-week periods in two different placements, and each period is followed by an intensive one-week seminar on campus, where the students bring back case studies and analyze them with their classmates.

Maryville, like most of the other sites in my study, goes "through the back door" to find its placement sites and cooperating teachers (co-ops), and it is painstaking work. "It takes us three to five years to develop a site," says Elizabeth Wren. "A friend who is a CEO is amazed by the complexity of what we do."

Most co-ops are former Maryville graduate students, but they are specifically trained for their role. "Some master teachers [in the schools] aren't very good at explaining what they do, and many hate to give up control," says Nicole Stewart of the education department. The university requires co-ops to take a course, at no cost, designed to help them become effective mentors. In addition, they are given tuition vouchers for another course at the university.

Most Maryville faculty members are engaged in the clinical supervision of students. By conventional standards, the supervision is intensive. Faculty members work with only five or six students at a time and are therefore able to observe and critique them frequently. In addition, the university provides opportunities for its student teachers to meet with other Maryville graduates who are teaching in the area.

Before Maryville graduates its students, they must go through an exit interview and make a presentation to the faculty, which usually involves the enactment of a sequence of lessons, followed by an analysis of the strengths and weaknesses of the lessons. The adequacy of the candidate's self-critique is the test of whether the student has acquired the maturity for honest assessment of his or her own work.

A few years ago, the state legislature, prodded by Wren, mandated that first- and second-year teachers be followed up by their teacher education institutions. Maryville, however, is the only institution in the state whose education faculty actually spend time in the schools and classrooms, since the Maryville administration agreed to release faculty members from one course each term in order to comply with the law.

Math Methods

In an elementary math methods course taught by Katherine Doyle, the intellectual demands are high. If I had merely watched, I would have thought that the tasks were demeaning in their simplicity. Since I was paired with a student, however, and went through the exercises myself, I could see the complexity and challenges of the work.

My partner and I worked on a series of exercises involving loops of cord and plastic tiles in three colors, four shapes, and two sizes. We each took turns sorting the tiles—first according to binary criteria, and then according to overlapping criteria—and then, by asking questions to which the other could reply only yes or no, tried to discover the other's criteria. The object was to discover the other person's reasoning with as few questions as possible. For some of the twosomes in the class, the exercise was rough going. Either the first partner misconceived the task or the second partner could not grasp the pattern through trial and error. Some of the women in the class seemed bewildered—surprised by how difficult the task was, and then paralyzed with embarrassment over their inability to do work that little kids could do. It was not child's play, however. It was hard analytic work. In the subsequent class discussion, the professor drew out the implications of the exercise for mathematics, science, social science, and logic.

In another exercise, we estimated the number of jelly beans in a jar. Although it was fun, I could not see the point, and so I asked Katherine Doyle about the exercise's purpose.

"I'll bet that when you go grocery shopping, you estimate how much your bill will be," she said, "rounding up and rounding down as you throw items into your cart. I'll bet that you estimate whether you will have enough money in your checking account to finish out the month. I'll bet that you estimate whether you have enough gasoline to get to the next exit on the highway. When you use a calculator, I'll bet that you run a mental tally to check your results."

I sheepishly admitted to doing all those things. As I did, I realized that I had spent a lifetime keeping those mental calculations half outside my awareness. From that moment on, I have made my estimating more conscious. As Doyle predicted, my estimating skill has improved dramatically. Perhaps like others in the class, I had not recognized these householder ruminations as mathematics.

I was exhilarated by Professor Doyle's teaching. She lectured only intermittently. Otherwise, she kept me spellbound with mathematical problems. She presented information that was crucial to future teachers but that never would have been presented in an academic mathematics class.

In a later interview, I asked Doyle why some of the students did not seem to be "getting it." Were they so wedded to rule-bound mathematics that they could not process what was happening?

"Before they graduate, most of them will move to at least a baseline understanding of this approach to mathematics and teaching," she said. As a first step, Doyle tries to get her students to reconsider what mathematics is; after attending only one of Doyle's classes, I myself came to see mathematics in a new light. Many of the difficulties that people have with mathematics occur at the intersection between language and mathematics, and so Doyle requires her students to talk and write about mathematics. Nevertheless, says Doyle, some students do not score well enough in the basic mathematics classes or in the math methods class to stay in the program. But mathematics is not the only snag. "If they cannot write, don't read, can't analyze, or don't have a good enough grade point average, they don't go on," says Doyle.

A Tough Course in Educational Psychology

Taylor Blount, one of the four men in the division, teaches two courses in developmental psychology to preservice teachers and graduate students in education. The courses encompass and integrate developmental and educational psychology. Blount is known in the department as the most assiduous maintainer of standards. He assigns a lot of writing and expects students' papers to be coherent, grammatical, and typographically correct. As a "constructivist" teacher, he usually refuses to give his students "the answer" and forces them to struggle with questions. He is a hard grader.

When I asked Blount about his grading policy, he said, "I struggle with the question 'Should this person become a teacher?' Would I want my child taught by this person? Also, I ask myself if it is fair to make a judgment about a twenty-year old."

Blount uses literature (*King Lear, Brave New World, A Tree Grows in Brooklyn*) as well as social science data to nudge his students into an examination of their viewpoints. For example, he challenges older women with traditional views on gender roles, as well as "mindless daycare-dependent professionals," to reconsider their assumptions.

In class, Blount seemed to be trying to jolt his students out of their passivity and nearly mortal fear of disagreement. He requires students to debate important issues in class, and he often directs students to make the case for positions they reject. For the first fifteen minutes of class, I observed a small group preparing the pro-choice position for an upcoming class debate on abortion. A young nun-in-training had been assigned to this group and seemed to be getting into the spirit of the task.

For the rest of the hour, Blount lectured on stages of cognitive development. Although this kind of theoretical, jargon-laden material is the sort that education bashers love to deride, most of the students I later interviewed said that it was extremely useful. Teachers constantly run the risk of pitching their lessons too low or too high, of boring the fast kids or confusing the slow ones, or of failing to situate a problem in a context that means something to students of a given age. Without theoretical grounding in the stages of cognitive development, the psychology of learning, and the techniques associated with various learning theories, teachers may fail to detect when and why students have not understood what was taught. They may underestimate or overestimate the time it takes to teach a topic—both disastrous errors. Or they may fail to recognize that it is time to move on or try another tack. Teachers trained at Maryville, like others I spoke to elsewhere, like to cite instances when they got past rough spots in teaching by remembering what they had learned about educational psychology.

Who's Responsible for Teaching Teachers to Write?

A visit to the first meeting of a methods course for prospective teachers of literature and writing revealed a breakdown between the English and education programs. The professor, Nicole Stewart, asked the students to talk about their own writing and reading habits. With few exceptions, the students in this class had not done and did not do any writing—not even letters or diary entries. Many found the memory of school-induced writing painful. Yet here was a group of women who would become teachers of writing.

When I asked Stewart about this crucial deficiency, she sighed and said that she wished the English faculty would "hold the line" on grades in freshman composition courses. "We require students to earn a B in freshman comp before being admitted to the education program, but nearly everybody gets a B. When they come to us, many of them can't write, and they say they didn't do much writing in their composition classes. We require a lot of writing in the teacher education program, and we arrange tutorials for the ones who are really poor, but the division of education shouldn't be responsible for teaching students to write. We have enough to do teaching them how to *teach* writing and literature."

The division's faculty are also frustrated with the history department. Unable to find historiography within the courses offered, the education division suggested to the history department that such a course be developed and offered within the education division. The history department did agree to offer the course, but development of the syllabus, readings, and experiential components has fallen to the education division.

Even on a small campus like Maryville's where professors in all departments work in close proximity, face-to-face contact and friendly persuasion may not resolve the discontinuity between academic and professional education. Here, as elsewhere, teacher educators lack the clout to hold arts and sciences faculty accountable.

A Passionate Pedagogue in Physics

I discovered a refreshing counterexample when I interviewed Corinne Wagner, a professor of physics. She teaches a course in physical science that fulfills a state requirement. Maryville's education division mandates this course, along with geology and biology, for all its education students. When I asked Wagner about the level of her students' mathematical knowledge—usually a stumbling block for physics students in both high school and college—she said, "Physics can be taught on many mathematical levels. There is no reason why students can't enjoy the study of nature at lesser levels of mathematical sophistication. You can teach the concepts graphically, or you can teach them with calculus. Even those who are good at calculus often find the graphics more useful to their understanding. The important thing is to understand the concepts, which I try to relate to the real world."

Wagner's zeal for teaching those who are not conventionally prepared is in marked contrast to the attitudes I see in most high school and college physics teachers, who tend to drive students out if they are not up to snuff in calculus. Wagner can hardly contain her delight in physics, in the teaching of it. She switched on a computer to show me a program designed to teach the distinction between velocity and acceleration.

"I have to stand on my head to teach it so that the students get it," she said, "so I present physical experiments, video realizations, and computer analogues. I have a whole bagful of concrete examples and exhibits that I interweave with abstractions."

Wagner, one of the Sacred Heart nuns still teaching at Maryville, did her doctoral work in education and specialized in cognitive structures and the application of critical thinking to physics and engineering problems. Clearly, she is a deep pedagogical thinker—just the kind needed to teach a subject that many students find intimidating, especially women students gripped with anxiety about science.

Later, I happened on a first-year teacher of third graders who had studied physics with Wagner. She said she learned a lot, not only about physics but also about teaching. "We did a lot of experiments, and her explanations were very clear. I admire her willingness to change explanations to suit the questioner."

Wagner does not have a Ph.D. in physics, which probably would make her suspect in the eyes of most science faculties. Yet the pipeline for future physicists is drying up because so many students are defeated by the subject's apparent difficulty. One might ask who is most likely to produce more future physicists—Wagner, or a more conventional physics professor?

Multiculturalism at Maryville

Blacks are a submerged group in the city of St. Louis, where Maryville is. The evening public TV programs I watched in my hotel room revealed a lot of tension over black unemployment and the allocation of political power. From the downcast look of many blacks I saw on the streets, it seemed to me that the "black is beautiful" movement had never reached this city. St. Louis seems to combine the worst of traditional Southern attitudes about race with the black despair seen in "rust bucket" cities in the Midwest.

Just before I went to Maryville, there had been a racial incident on campus. Somebody had spray-painted racial epithets on the window of a black student's dormitory room, and the faculty had been in a sweat to find the right response. But before any proscriptions against hate speech could be entertained or approved, the

Black Student Association—a very small group—had called a campuswide meeting, and many white students showed up. Tensions seem to ease because those who attended were able to speak freely.

I sat in on a meeting between a professor and an African-American evaluation consultant. The two were designing a plan to improve the preparation of Maryville's students to teach in multicultural settings. The focus of the plan is on attitudes, on the effects of bigotry on teaching and learning, and on the provision of experiences that would expose Maryville undergraduates to the precocity of black middle-class students, in order to blast common stereotypes. The planners envisioned a program to have teacher education students "shadow" a young, angry black male in the city, as a way of gaining immediate knowledge that just having black skin can make everything more difficult—job applications, purchases, and flat tires.

The Maryville plan would tuck some pieces of the desired cultural and historical knowledge into the appropriate liberal arts courses. Maryville's planners were already talking to arts and sciences faculty about the inclusion of black history and culture in existing courses. The history of St. Louis and the civil rights movement would be included in a sophomore "foundations" course in the division of education.

As is true elsewhere, Maryville's education faculty feel the urgency of changing teachers' attitudes about race and culture, but they are somewhat unsure of how to proceed. The depth and duration of racism in the United States, the recent memory of hopeful reforms and dashed hopes, and the frailty of knowledge about how to change adult attitudes, make them cautious.

Out in the Schools

Marcie worked as a waitress for sixteen years, then as a dental assistant, but ultimately decided to prepare for teaching. She went to Maryville because she had heard good things about it. Once there, she found the coursework rigorous. She took astronomy, chemistry, and algebra and had to do a lot of writing, which she struggled with at first. Now she keeps a journal.

As a student teacher in a second-grade class, she is grateful for the training she had in classroom management. She learned most of what she knows about managing kids in her sophomore year, when she got ideas and coaching from her supervising professor and became more conscious of what she was doing by keeping a journal.

She believes that the public's image of teachers is beginning to improve, but she is less sure about school administrators' image of teachers: "Teachers don't have any input, and the male administrators make all the decisions." She foresees herself becoming "somewhat feisty" in the future about teachers' role in curriculum and policy decisions—once she has tenure.

Helen is now a full-fledged teacher, having graduated from Maryville last year. She too is grateful for her pedagogical training: "I would have had *many* more problems this year without that training, but because of it, I knew what to look for." She is pleased that her college teachers come by to visit twice a year. Like Marcie, she shows signs of assertiveness. She disciplined a child who was doing his math homework during her science class, and when his parents complained to the school, she held her ground. She also reports that the people in her social circle respect school teachers.

Betty, a practice teacher at another elementary school, thinks that the way math is taught now is a big improvement over the way it was taught to her, when teachers' focus was on what she had done wrong. In her math methods courses, she learned not only how to do mathematics but also how to explain it to other adults and to children: "My kids do a lot of talking about math, as well as writing. At first, I wondered whether the kids would learn as much. Now I see that they know more than I did."

Julie, who is doing her practice teaching in an upscale school district, showed uncommon wisdom in the handling of a little tyrant. When the presence of the word *fart* in some reading material caused the class to laugh, the student thought that the class was laughing at him, and he had an asthma attack. In the nurse's office, the student blamed the practice teacher for not handling the situation the way the regular teacher would have done, and he demanded that all the other kids be punished. While declining to obey his order, Julie worked out an arrangement with the child. Now when he has an asthma attack, he is supposed to step out of the room. Meanwhile, she is trying to discover the child's strengths and interests and find out who he wants his friends to be.

The high school teachers I interviewed were equally emphatic about the value of pedagogical training. Sam, a student teacher in English, had a friend with a master's degree in French, who was teaching in a private school and having a hard time. Henri asked Sam to come and observe.

"Classroom management was Henri's biggest problem," Sam said. "He was trying to recreate the experience he had as a student in France: teachers lecture, students listen, take notes, do assignments, and turn in perfect papers or else suffer low grades. Henri was surprised when students talked. He was impatient with students who had learning disabilities and would have seen any adjustment of his lesson plans to their needs as a lowering of standards. He was bribing the students with promises of reduced work in exchange for their listening and working."

Sam gave Henri a theoretical perspective on discipline and on learning-disabled students. He then taught three of Henri's classes, to demonstrate negative and positive reinforcement, extinguishing of unwanted behavior, and the importance of clear teaching objectives.

The teachers I interviewed were responding to my questions: "How do you rate your college education?" and "What was useful, and what was a waste of time?" Perhaps Maryville's courses, like Trinity's, are more practical and substantive than those taken twenty years ago by the vociferous critics of methods courses. Perhaps the material has more meaning because these teachers are simultaneously observing its use by experienced teachers and applying it to their own practice teaching. Perhaps their education professors, who are teaching as they hope their students will teach, help them absorb and appropriate what they learn verbally.

Making the Right Connections

The Maryville teacher education program is not a collection of courses required for teacher certification. It is a thoughtful attempt to integrate the many components of a good preparation program. The struggle to connect subject matter with pedagogy of subject matter is difficult. As at Trinity University and the University of Texas at San Antonio the cooperation of academic faculty depends more on the attitudes and teaching ability of individual professors than on institutional incentives, support, and sanctions. In its attempt to construct the all-important connection between campus learning and the practice of teaching, Maryville's education program must tiptoe around the public school power structure and supply most of the energy and initiative. Even though the Maryville division of education exists in a society that systematically underestimates the complexity of teaching, it has made prodigious efforts to create for its students a seamless garment of knowledge, principles, and experience and to strike the Archimedean point between compassion and standards.

5

The Impact of
State-level Reform

At Portland State University, a refreshingly practical and
sharply focused graduate program for future teachers mir-
rors a daring and comprehensive state education-reform
plan. All eyes are on the application of academic studies
to jobs in a fluid, global economy.

Teacher education in its traditional form is beginning to disappear
in Oregon. In 1991, the two largest public universities in the state
summarily abolished—without consulting officials in elementary
and secondary education—most of their undergraduate teacher
preparation programs. These actions by university leaders were
foreshadowed by general dissatisfaction with old-style teacher education and spurred by severe budget constraints in higher education.
This abrupt termination of two major education programs occurred
on the cusp of the legislature's overhaul of the entire precollege
educational system in the state, embodied in a new state law.

Despite howls of protest from the state's school leaders, who
had been counting on the universities to retool their teacher education programs in accordance with the state's radically revised
goals, it now appears that the coincidence of higher education's

retreat and the public schools' rejuvenation will be a happy one. The time-encrusted education schools are disappearing, and new ones are being created around very different premises. Here, more than in other states, it is possible to see how a state's philosophy of education and its goals for students determine the shape and direction of teacher education. To put this matter another way, schools of education are creatures of the school systems they serve.

Teacher Education in a Revolutionary Context

Portland State University (PSU) is now at the center of gravity in teacher education in Oregon. To understand the content and character of PSU's somewhat atypical approach to teacher education, one must understand Oregon's education-reform plan, which in turn is embedded in a grand plan that touches nearly every aspect of life. The state has mounted an all-out assault on the entire interlocking array of social, health, educational, economic, and environmental problems. In 1989, the state developed a twenty-year strategic vision, embodied in a report that portrays a state seeking and expecting to get a high quality of life. Out of that report grew the Progress Board, which developed a comprehensive set of measurable standards to be met by the years 1995, 2000, and 2010. For example, social benchmarks for the next five years include such items as a sharp reduction in the rate of teen pregnancies and adult illiteracy and the near-elimination of drug use by teenagers. Economic benchmarks include such items as a dramatic increase in the percentage of lumber- and wood-products manufacturing employees in "value-added manufacturing" (Oregon wants to enjoy the full economic benefit of its lumber, rather than ship it out of state for others to convert into wood products). Quality-of-life benchmarks include all the state's residents living where the air meets government air-quality standards.

Oregon's planners were responding to warning signals: a decline in the forest-products industry as the timber harvest shrinks, the flight of low-skilled jobs to developing countries, a higher percentage of low-birth-weight babies, explosive growth in the number of drug-addicted mothers, an increased percentage of children in poverty and "unresponsive first graders," a large percentage of high school dropouts, a sharp rise in juvenile delinquency, and an exploding prison population.

Portland State University and the Spirit of Reform

PSU began as a community college, evolved into a city college, and is now on its way to becoming a full-service university. In this transition, the university has benefited from the financial distress of Oregon's more prestigious campuses. As tuition at those schools went up, so did enrollments at the less expensive Portland State. When the other schools closed most of their education programs, in 1991, Portland State's department of education inherited a flood of applicants. PSU has abolished the undergraduate degree in education and now offers only a master's degree program, which has attracted a good many older adults with extensive work background and community experience, as well as practicing teachers who want to position themselves for the reforms while earning advanced degrees. The average age of the students is thirty-four.

The popularity of Portland State's education program is attributable not only to its urban location and lower tuition but also to its growing reputation for liveliness and quality. Portland State's education faculty have enthusiastically embraced the spirit of the reform movement. Says Wesley Campion, acting chair of the department of education, "We studied the new law for the criticisms of teacher education inherent in it; we have used this legislation as an opportunity to do the things we should have been doing much earlier." Department faculty use the teaching methods that they expect their students to use in the schools. There is an emphasis on cooperative learning and applied academics. Among those who teach in the department of education, the ability to exert a positive influence on teaching practice is more valued than publishing, and the administration concurs.

Students go through the program in "cohorts" of twenty-five to thirty, taking classes together half the time and spending the other half working together in clusters of schools. "Teachers have never been trained to work in teams, but under the new law they will have to work that way," says Campion. Cultural diversity is also a theme of the new law; therefore, PSU practice teachers are placed in inner-city schools as well as suburban schools, to increase their awareness of the needs of students from varying groups and settings.

The cohort approach provides team members with a strong support system and allows the faculty to design the program for each cohort around a theme. "Work-force issues" was the theme for a secondary teacher education cohort in the spring of 1992. Participants were screened for their ability to contribute to the group's knowledge about a variety of occupations. Another cohort group sent teacher candidates out in pairs to work in social service agencies, churches, recreation programs, police stations, and probation offices. They went to these assignments with a question not often asked by educators: "What advice do you have for teachers?" A middle school project sponsored by another cohort sent pupils out to discover what it took to run the businesses on the commercial strip across from the school. The kids studied the operations of a drugstore, a grocery store, a dry-cleaning establishment, and other businesses on the strip. In the process, students learned to apply mathematics, social studies, and communication skills to the study of these businesses, and they learned a lot about the adults in their community.

Portland State has also created a reform-oriented advanced-degree program for school administrators. The program's reputation for excellence has spread. Aspiring principals who once might have enrolled elsewhere are now flocking to Portland State.

Science Education at Portland State

Craig Coe is a veteran high school science teacher who became a professor of science education at Portland State. Like many other exemplary high school teachers, Coe is warm, practical, and plain-spoken. His background as a high school teacher in Portland is an enormous asset in matching student teachers with cooperating teachers. "We have a lot of good science teachers in the schools, and I know many of them," says Coe. "I get to know all my students very well, so that I can usually make a good match with the cooperating teachers."

Coe acknowledges the subject matter deficiencies of teachers but sees many more gaps in math and science knowledge among elementary teachers than among secondary teachers. He thinks that many education courses are indeed a waste of time (media courses, for example); nevertheless, he believes that pedagogical training is important for all teachers. "Without pedagogy, the kids will eat you alive. The pedagogy most missing is experience. Teachers don't know what students are going to find difficult. When they check for understanding, they often find that the kids don't understand. Often teachers merely repeat an explanation. I teach them to ask a student who *did* get it to explain it to the others. That way, teachers get a new set of explanations that are effective with kids."

I observed one of Coe's evening classes of graduate students. Most of them are science teachers in Portland schools. Coe began by telling them how much he enjoyed reading the papers they had written about a role-playing game that extends over five class periods and exposes students to the conflicting ecological, sociological, and political issues involved in environmental planning. "I could feel their emotion," Coe told the class, uttering a word ordinarily forbidden in academic discourse.

The class then discussed some of the tricky issues in cooperative learning: how to make sure all students participate, how to structure tasks so that kids who prefer to play supportive roles can do so, how to give groups extra credit for behavior and decorum as well as for "winning," what to do with kids who, on religious grounds, do not want to participate in a creation versus evolution debate (ask them to be judges and to mark down points for rule violations).

Then, in a collegial manner, students took turns presenting materials and projects that they had developed for their junior and senior high classes. Some presentations stimulated enthusiastic responses from class members. There was a scheme that brought science students and vocational education students together to work on a salmon-enhancement project. There was also a class recycling project that met its goal of reducing the school's garbage by one dumpster per week. That goal had required students to learn how to organize a complicated effort and persuade unmotivated people to cooperate.

Portland's science education program highlights the idea

that a broader range of people will have to be recruited into teaching. Teachers will need to go beyond merely knowing their subjects. They must be able to imagine how knowledge is applied and help their students situate knowledge in practical contexts.

The Oregon Plan for Education

Even for education alone, the state's plan is a plateful. It includes more emphasis on the following elements:

- Academic preparation of teachers
- State-funded mentors for beginning teachers
- Official encouragement for school-site management
- Phased-in expansion of early childhood programs for all preschoolers
- A shift toward ungraded primary schools
- A curriculum aimed at the preparation of a high-wage, highly skilled work force
- An emphasis on applied academics
- A shift from standardized paper-and-pencil tests to performance tests
- School choice for students who are not prospering in their local schools
- The infusion of multicultural studies
- Foreign-language instruction for everyone
- Gradual lengthening of the school year
- A shift in teaching methods, to emphasize students' ability to work in teams, think, and solve real-world problems
- Closer relationships with parents
- Coordination of social agencies and schools
- Forging of new alliances with community colleges, technical institutes, and the business community

The plan incorporates nearly every aspect of schooling.

Disappointment with the results of school reforms in the 1980s explains Oregon's rejection of an incremental strategy and its preference for an all-at-once strategy. In the mid-1980s, Oregon, like most other states, tried to reform education by mandating higher test scores. In 1984, researcher Patricia Cross predicted the outcome of such a strategy:

> The curriculum will be tidied up, goals will be artic-
> ulated, standardized tests will control transitions from
> one level of schooling to another, prospective teachers
> will study a core of common learnings, and the teacher
> education curriculum will be restructured to include
> certain experiences in specified sequences. There is
> not much evidence that the current mania for tidiness
> will produce orderly schools in which students and
> teacher pursue learning with the contagious enthusi-
> asm that is so essential for excellence.[1]

As predicted, state manipulation of the existing system did not produce the intended results. As the economy declined and pressure to
reform the schools increased, Oregon's leaders became aware that
the 1980s-style incremental reforms were insufficient.

As state leaders leaders began to fashion the second wave of
education reform, they were persuaded by Marc Tucker, president
of the National Center on Education and the Economy, that real
change would occur only when the schools were restructured to give
teachers a more powerful voice in decisions about how to educate
students. Legislative translations of Tucker's convictions began in
1987, with the passage of a law that supported pilot projects in
school restructuring and school-site decision making and established the Beginning Teacher Support Program, which trains and
pays experienced teachers to mentor first-year teachers. The second
piece of reform legislation occurred in 1989, with a bill designed to
stimulate innovation at local schools by excusing them from some
(but not all) state and local regulations. The third and most comprehensive education-reform package is embodied in the new law
passed in 1991. That law presumes that virtually all citizens need
to prepare for a high-skills, high-wage economy.

In making the commitment to "meet international standards
in key occupations and industries," Oregon intends to prepare its
youth for changes in job requirements that have not yet taken place.
For that reason, the plan is not narrowly vocational. Since the exact

nature of job requirements cannot be foreseen, "the state's job is to prepare students for whatever the future holds," says Dale Parnell, commissioner of community colleges and author of *The Neglected Majority*.[2] The mathematical, scientific, verbal, and social under-pinnings of highly skilled technical work are the focus of the state's approach to vocational education.

Oregon is the first state to respond to the long-uttered criticism that the schools send the bottom half of the population out on the streets with minimal academic skills and nothing much to do except wander from one minimum-wage job to another. Students who do not flourish in the didactic, passive, abstract college-preparatory program (the vast majority) are seen as failures in most school systems. Many drop out. Those who remain are usually relegated to the undemanding "general track," which Oregon will abolish, or to narrow programs in vocational education, which the state will replace with "applied academics."

The Oregon education plan has attracted criticism from advocates of traditional classical education, who believe that vocational emphasis will lead to neglect of the humanities. The plan has also attracted criticism from those whose are concerned about equity. These critics see in the Oregon plan an attempt to replicate the practice, common in European countries, of separating the "sheep" from the "goats" prematurely. The higher education community in particular has resisted the idea of giving high school students the option of choosing a technical career. According to one state official, "College people don't want students to decide what to do until late college, and they think the schools will be forcing students into early decisions. The subtext here is that the people from the colleges and universities are worried about losing students to the community colleges."

Certificate of Initial Mastery

By the end of the 1996–97 school year, Oregon students who are sixteen or have completed the tenth grade will have the opportunity to qualify for a Certificate of Initial Mastery, comparable to the British O-levels examination. This feature of the plan, along with many others, is derived from the highly influential 1990 report from the National Center on Education and the Economy, *America's Choice: High Skills or Low Wages.*[3]

Standards for the Certificate of Initial Mastery will not be formalized until 1995, but the legislation calls for competence in reading, writing, mathematics, science, foreign languages, and the arts. In these academic studies, however, the tilt will be toward application rather than memorization, and toward interdisciplinary approaches rather than compartmentalized subject matter. In addition, students will be expected to exhibit the capacity to learn, think, reason, retrieve information, and work effectively alone and in groups. Oregon benchmarks for education call for students to rank first in the nation by the year 2000 in national assessments of geography, history, math, reading, science, and writing and, by the year 2021, to reach "world class" standards. Also by 2021, 55 percent of Oregon's high school graduates are to be enrolled in some form of advanced technical education.

Students who do not meet Oregon's new academic standards by the age of sixteen will be encouraged to attend learning centers, where they will continue their education until they meet the standards or turn twenty-one.

Certificate of Advanced Mastery

Students who earn a Certificate of Initial Mastery will have several options. One will be work-based learning, for those who want to enter the work force immediately. These students will be provided some combination of work-oriented study and supervised work experience, and they will be permitted to reenter the educational system at a later date. The vast majority of students, however, will enroll in one of three programs leading to a Certificate of Advanced Mastery, with "endorsements" in a standard college preparation program or in the technical professional associate degree (TPAD) program, a professional technical-preparation degree program that spans the last two years of high school and two years in a community college or technical institute.

While still in high school, students in the TPAD program may choose from among six career options: arts and communications, health services, business and management, human resources, industry and technology, and natural resources. Courses in mathematics, science, English, and the social sciences will be designed to support the careers that students think they want to pursue. State education officials are determined to leave the future open for these students, however. They are now seeking approval for these courses from the state's higher education system, so that students in TPAD courses can gain admission to traditional college programs if they change their minds. Approval has already been granted for several courses.

Oregon's planners believe that many students in college-track programs will ultimately prefer applied academic courses because these are more immediately relevant and engaging. Difficult subjects, such as mathematics and physics, are easier to master when presented in context: "Most people know that it is simply better teaching," says Dale Parnell. The community college phase of the program will involve both academic study and apprenticeships.

Can Oregon Pull It Off?

"If it can't be done here, it can't be done anywhere," says Marcia Franklin, the state's associate superintendent for public instruction, referring to the relative absence of social and economic problems and the state's history of high public support for public services. Nevertheless, realizing the plan's goals will be staggeringly complicated, even if Oregon taxpayers have the funds to support those goals and the willingness to spend the necessary money.

Time and money are the most crucial factors in achieving the plan's goals. The existing cadre of teachers, as well as prospective teachers, must be trained to teach in an entirely different way. Teachers must have time during the school day to work together designing new curricula, to plan a more complex program, to learn new pedagogy, and to reflect on what they are doing. A longer school day and school year seem necessary, and those are the most expensive items.

Oregon's strategy for the reform of teacher education bears the stamp of a particular moment in American educational history—the moment when the Holmes Group report *Tomorrow's Teachers* (1986) defined "rigor" as a bachelor's degree in a traditionally taught university program, followed by a fifth-year master's-degree program combining the study of pedagogy with field experience. The Holmes Group now disavows that simplistic interpretation of rigor and calls for a different kind of teaching in the academic disciplines, as well as for better integration of content, pedagogy, and field experience throughout the college years.

If Oregon is to achieve its own goals, it will need to retrace its steps in order to reconnect undergraduate studies in the academic disciplines and the pedagogical arts—a connection that is especially important for the success of applied academics and teaching for understanding. For example, in a system where a physics teacher should know how to take apart a small engine in order to illustrate the principles of mechanics, the traditionally abstract presentation of academic disciplines will not serve the goals of the plan, and so the abandonment of teacher education by Oregon's research universities may turn out to be a blessing in disguise. Community and regional colleges, which make no claims to exalted reputations for research, may be far more fertile ground for developing innovative courses in the arts and sciences and for connecting academic disciplines to pedagogy and work.

The state's 1991 law is appealing in its boldness and vision. Elsewhere, educators and the public have been lamenting the failure of the schools to meet the academic and vocational needs of students who do not plan to go to college. Oregon has a well-conceived, serious plan to educate those students. No other state has approached this issue with such seriousness.

Nevertheless, the new law represents a dizzying array of initiatives and includes a pastiche of old ideas in new garb. "Developmentally appropriate education," which is what Oregon intends to achieve with ungraded primary schools, has become a slippery slope to low expectations in the places where it has been tried. Moreover, recent research shows that there is a down side to cooperative learning. It is desperately difficult to design inherently instructive tasks for small groups. There is also evidence that groups formed for cooperative learning tend to replicate the existing social pecking order, with a vengeance. Many features of Oregon's plan seem to have been lifted intact from the National Center on Education and the Economy's 1990 report, but that report works better as a futurist vision than as a strategic plan for altering a complex, change-resistant institution.

The notion of teaching for understanding and application is incontestably valid. Why would anyone prefer teaching that does not result in students' understanding or ability to apply knowledge? But this better kind of teaching cuts against the grain of educational history. The idea of simply putting out the information, leaving to fate and genetics whether students "get it," is deeply embedded in our culture. Besides, versions of "teaching for understanding" have been tried before and did not last long. Most important, the kind of teaching Oregon envisions depends on radical transformation in the way the disciplines are typically taught in colleges. The state must devise powerful incentives for improved teaching in undergraduate liberal arts programs.

According to Miles Soutier, a middle school teacher in the state capital, the state's teachers are worried about betrayal of the promise to hold off on implementing the reforms unless there is enough money to carry them out properly. Soutier says that Oregon's teachers are tired of gearing up for the "mandate of the year," which some legislator heard about at a conference and later pushed into law, only to have the same mandate rescinded the following year. Also, Soutier says, some features of the plan seem inconsistent with others; for example, the mandate to involve parents in their children's education is hard to reconcile with the new approach to mathematics. Like parents who struggled with "new math" a generation ago, today's parents, says Soutier, will be at a loss to understand another alien conception of mathematics.

The shift to applied academics presumes that state taxpayers are willing to pay for serious efforts in staff development for existing teachers. In that respect, Oregon's leaders are optimistic. There is a good chance that the legislature will let the state superintendent have discretionary funds for in-service training. Moreover, the state expects to claim some of the $100 million in federal funds designated for programs that combine academic and vocational education.

Implications for Teacher Education

The Oregon plan for school reform will require teachers who are skilled in teaching students to work in groups and apply their knowledge to real-world tasks. Equipping teachers for these new roles is a tall order, however, because the lecture-assignment-test format is deeply rooted, and because "hands on" work has never been wholly embraced by the educational system and those who enter it. The successful management of cooperative learning requires a deep understanding of its theory and much guided practice. Teachers will need a richer, more conceptual understanding of subject matter and much more real-world experience in order to design lessons that not only teach academic skills but also allow students to apply their knowledge to problems worth solving.

Time will tell whether Oregon has bitten off more than it can chew and, if so, whether it can define achievable interim steps that build on one another. Even if some of the elements of this bold vision fail to materialize, there is still the hope that some of the more promising features will survive because they respond to authentic economic and social needs and lay the foundation for better teacher education, better teaching, and a better future for the state's citizens.

6

New Pedagogies, Old Environments

Even the most elegant, efficient design for integrating all aspects of teachers' education and training—knowledge of the disciplines, knowledge about how to teach those disciplines, and knowledge of the great variety of students to be educated—may be diminished if the college environment and the political climate of the community are basically unfriendly to teachers.

Millersville University, just outside the city of Lancaster, is in the heart of the Pennsylvania Dutch country. The university began as a normal school in 1859—the first normal school in the state—and has evolved into a full-service state university offering degrees and graduate programs in a variety of disciplines and professions. It is one of fourteen such institutions in the state system of higher education. The vast majority of its students come from nearby counties, where the population is overwhelmingly white, prosperous, hardworking, and conservative.

Nearly half of Millersville's four thousand students are enrolled in the school of education. Of those, about 38 percent are undergraduates or postbaccalaureate students earning credits for teacher certification. The elementary education majors, as a group, have the highest SAT scores and the highest grade-point averages in the university. (Admission to the university requires a minimum 950 SAT score; admission to the elementary education program requires a minimum of 1050 on the SAT.) In addition, two arts and science faculty members must give their approval for a student to enter the education program. "They are able students and they do well on tests," says Barry Hart, acting dean of the school of education.

Future teachers must take a hefty academic program. Students are required to do a lot of writing in both their academic and professional courses. There is evidence that many courses in the education program are rigorous too. The math methods course, which several students told me was more difficult than the calculus course, washes a number of students out of the program.

Fusing Content and Pedagogy

The most remarkable feature of teacher education at Millersville is the extent to which the program has created a synthesis of subject matter and pedagogy. In 1988, under the leadership of Amanda Kirk, pedagogy seminars came into being. These seminars, which earn students one academic credit, are held once a week at a mutually convenient time for members of the class. Before the seminar meets, students turn in notes they have taken after each of their three-times-weekly classes in subject matter. The course professor and a professor of education review the notes before the seminar meets and prepare responses to students' questions and critiques.

In the seminars, students become students of their own learning, as well as students of the professor's teaching. They explore how they themselves are learning the course material and pinpoint things the professor does that help or hinder their learning. "Everything about the professor's teaching is fair game," says Amanda Kirk. A student can say to a professor, "If you had stopped before that last example, I wouldn't have understood what you were talking about." The professor explains why he organized the course as he did, and why he tests as he does. Students begin to analyze the kinds of subject matter knowledge that will be useful to them as teachers and to generate metaphors, examples, analogies, explana-tions, models, and other strategies for reaching the minds of their future students. Students who have experienced pedagogy seminars in more than one subject begin to think about teaching strategies in one subject that can be applied usefully to another.

With the pedagogy seminars under way, Millersville was poised to apply for funds from Project 30, an effort to encourage the integration of subject matter and pedagogy, supported by the Car-negie Foundation. In 1989, Millersville was accepted for participa-tion on the basis of the promising start it had made. Millersville also shared in a National Endowment for the Humanities (NEH) grant given to the American Association of Colleges to foster the integra-tion of the humanities into education programs. Recently, Millers-ville received its own NEH grant to support the creation of interdisciplinary courses that can be taken by any Millersville stu-dent but will be strongly recommended for education students. Since 1988, about sixty faculty members have team-taught these seminars, and thirty professors from arts and sciences have been involved in the effort. That thirty academic professors are willing to expose themselves to student critiques of their teaching is amaz-ing; equally amazing is that education students, with a history of obedience and grade-grubbing, would risk voicing their critiques. That students have the opportunity to think deeply about pedagogy in relation to content is a near-miracle.

Professor G. B. Edwards of the department of mathematics took part in a pedagogy seminar for a Calculus 2 course. "My students didn't have a lot of direct criticisms," he says, "but there were some indirect ones. Generally, I recognize it when my students aren't learning some larger topics in calculus, but I learned that I had messed up in a few small components of those topics. The students had to present lessons they would teach to their future stu-dents, and they endured a lot of criticism. One out of the eleven students in the class presented a lesson that was awful. The whole class got on board to help him understand why the lesson wasn't good, and he appreciated the criticism."

The existence of pedagogy seminars at Millersville can be explained by determined and skillful leadership—in this case, Amanda Kirk's. Moreover, the fact that the school of education enrolls half the students and that Millersville has a long tradition as an institution concerned with teaching suggests that the joining of content and pedagogy is more likely to happen in a university where the department of education enjoys more than the usual degree of respect and influence.

Standards Versus Grade Inflation

The integration of subject matter and pedagogy is far from complete, as seen in a recent episode on campus. Prodded by NCATE, the school of education attempted to raise the standard for admission to the school of education (in the sophomore year) from a grade-point average of 2.0 to one of 2.5, but the issue is currently stalled in the faculty senate. According to some education professors I interviewed, the science professors resisted the change because they thought that the education majors couldn't "make the grade." But, according to Harold Rosemann, an influential member of the science faculty and an ardent critic of teacher education, the faculty senate, especially those members from the department of mathematics, complained that the education department's decision had been made unilaterally, without the required consultation with the faculty senate. Professor Edwards made the same complaint. Faculty in the department of education, however, say that the school council and the provost have been aware of the proposed change for some time, and that academic departments had even identified the courses that would be subject to the 2.5 grade-point average. Whatever the truth of the matter, there are certainly differing perceptions of what constitutes "following procedures," as well as questions about whether the procedural complaints from academic professors mask other concerns.

One of those concerns, according to Rosemann, was ostensibly that some professors were worried that the change would lead to grade inflation (in order to "pass" students who want to become teachers), rather than to genuinely high standards.

"Wouldn't these same professors have to be the ones doing the inflating?" I asked Rosemann.

"The requirement for higher grades is across the board," he

said. "Students will need to earn higher grades in the humanities as well."

Earning grades in science and mathematics, however, seems to be the sticking point. One member of the education faculty said that the physics department enjoys giving low grades to education students. An education student who had made good grades in calculus, but found math methods more intellectually challenging, said, "The math department is out to get us."

I asked Rosemann if that were true. "Students get low grades when they can't meet the standards," he said. When I asked whether there is a mechanism for detecting patterns of high or low grading by professors, Rosemann said that he did "look at the grades."

Without a full-fledged research project, it is hard to know what is going on here. Do the mathematics and science professors really want "higher standards"? If so, why do they seem to resist the 2.5 standard on grounds that seem technical at best and bogus at worst? Are they worried about grade inflation within their own ranks, or only in the "softer" humanities departments? Is there a suspicion that their "high standards" are really a code phrase for "weeding out"? Whatever is happening at Millersville, national studies do show that physics professors quite often, and chemistry and math professors sometimes, see their job as sifting out the wheat from the chaff—the "wheat" being those who intend to become graduate students in the discipline.

At Millersville, as elsewhere, academic faculty members frequently complain that incoming students are unprepared, especially in science and mathematics. Edwards says that many of his calculus students were taught by high school teachers who "didn't know" calculus themselves, and who convinced their students that the subject is hard. Yet most of the calculus teachers in the area had received their training from the mathematics department at Millersville. Moreover, these calculus teachers would not have been accepted into the teacher education program unless members of the mathematics faculty had given their approval.

Amanda Kirk says that the department of education has been emphatic on this point: "Don't send them to us unless you believe they are prepared. If they can't do the work, we don't want them to be teachers." It seems, on the face of it, that the mathematics department, not the department of education, must take responsibility for the "unprepared" students that Edwards complains of.

James Rutherford is director of the American Academy for the Advancement of Science (AAAS) Project 2061, a long-range effort to improve precollege science and mathematics. According to him, physics and chemistry professors often "take high flunk rates as an indication that they are maintaining high standards." "High standards," Rutherford adds, often mean "science as I learned it."

Rosemann's assertion—"We should expect more of education students because their SAT scores are higher"—raises another question. Are SAT scores relevant to a student's success in college-level mathematics and science? Again, according to data from AAAS, there is a .5 correlation between SAT scores and students' college grades. If grades in science and mathematics were correlated with SAT scores, the correlation would be even lower.

In this vignette from Millersville, we can see one instance of a national dilemma in teacher education. "High standards" are more easily achieved rhetorically than practically. It is not a simple matter of requiring higher SAT scores or grade-point averages. Some professors patronize future teachers by giving them unearned grades, the better to reinforce their own belief that teachers are not very smart—or need not be very smart. Other professors give unearned grades to minority students, either in the belief that they are pressured to do so by higher-ups or out of the conviction that the schools need more minority teachers. Some professors get psychic jollies, or professional kudos, for being hard graders. Others reinforce their conviction that teachers are not very smart by flunking future teachers. The relationship between "high standards" as a rhetorical proposition, on the one hand, and the teaching and learning of content that is both rigorous and appropriate for future teachers, on the other, is exceedingly complex.

The resistance of the Millersville science faculty to a proposed reform seems curious, even irrational. The education school's proposal appears to respond to the assertion that future teachers should study science with "real" scientists, not science educators. The disdain of academics for teacher educators, however, is so deeply ingrained that even a reasonable idea seems contaminated merely by being proposed in the school of education. Academic scientists often do misconstrue their work as "teachers of teachers." Science educators, however, in entirely different ways, may also misconstrue their work and thus provide continuing justification for the academics' disdain. In the following vignette, we shall see how methods courses, even in a great school of education, can keep the feud going between academics and teacher educators.

A Science Methods Course

The students filter into a crowded classroom. At their benches, they find glass containers filled with a red liquid, as well as piles of paper towels. The professor asks the students to dip pieces of towel into the red liquid, observe how far the red liquid has traveled, and answer the day's question: "What force caused the water to move?"

Some students comment that the yellow component in the dye has moved to the outside edge of the blot, and that there is an olive-green blot in the center of the red spot. Other students notice that the liquid has moved up, while water usually falls down. A student identifies gravity as the downward force, and the professor writes "gravity" on the board under the caption "forces."

"Where, in life," asks the professor, "does this upward force of water occur?" Somebody says, "Straws." Another student says, "Siphons." The professor rejects both answers: "You have to *do* something, such as suck or pump, to start the upward motion."

The professor then offers "wick," as in a kerosene lamp, and "sponge," through which wax or water will move upward against the force of gravity. He asks the class to name the force. He is waiting for somebody to say the words "capillary action," which is the subject of the day's lesson, as yet unspoken by anyone.

One student says, nearly in a whisper, "Capillary tube, like the ones used in medicine to draw blood." But the professor ignores the half-right answer, still holding out for "capillary action." Moments pass, and nobody comes up with the right words. The professor hints that wicks are made of cotton, which is a natural fiber. Still nobody speaks. Even though these students have high SAT scores, have taken high school and college science courses, and no doubt have been exposed to the words *capillary* and *capillary action,* they are unwilling or unable to come up with what the professor wants.

Another hint: "This force works only in a small space," the professor says, "like capillary glass tubes in a hospital." Still no volunteers. Finally the professor offers the words "capillary action" and asks where else this principle works. One student, barely audible, says "The body." The professor asks whether blood in the body has to move against the force of gravity. Nobody answers. The professor prods, asking how the blood in the feet gets back up to the heart. Then he draws a tubular shape on the board and begins to describe capillary action in a small space. He shows how the two sides of the tube attract the molecules in the liquid, and how the shape of the liquid changes. He asks for the name of the shape: "Con . . . , con . . . ," he says, but nobody offers "concave," which was what he was hoping for.

The professor then asks, "Will your life be different now?" Nobody responds. "Your life will change only if you understand the implications of all this for real life, and for kids."

Finally, in a clear, assertive voice, a student asks a question about the connection of this experiment with a previous one on molecular movement in alcohol. The professor goes back to the board to explain molecular action.

The class then has ninety seconds to clean up after the red-liquid experiment and set up the work stations for the next experiment, which is meant to move the students, through induction, to a definition of "floating." Here again the students seem reluctant to answer the professor's repeated questions. He is trying to get the students to come up with conclusions based on observations in hands-on experiments, but it is not clear to me how the particular vocabulary words and definitions he has in mind can be reached inductively.

The professor in this case has incorporated most of the elements of good, constructivist teaching. But, like most other teachers around the nation, he is still working out the details of this kind of teaching, and it is very hard work. Although he provides concrete experiences with the materials of science, tries hard to draw on his students' existing knowledge, and aims to promote true understanding, the goals he seeks are diminished by his deeply ingrained habit of calling for the "right" answer.

Standards for the Education Faculty

As the preceding vignette illustrates, good teaching is complex and hard to codify. Nevertheless, Millersville education faculty have made a stab at defining standards for teaching in their own department. Education professors are expected to teach in the ways they expect their students to teach. They must do more than ask their students to memorize information. Instead, they must define tasks that call on students' capacity to reason about and apply information and that require students to work collaboratively. In the few classes I observed, the faculty appeared to be struggling against the passivity of their students.

As elsewhere, education faculty are expected to conduct and publish research on teaching and learning, but at Millersville the "publish or perish" rule is not inexorable. With its long tradition as a teacher-preparation institution, Millersville is primarily a teaching university. It is possible for a faculty member whose teaching is highly regarded, and who does community service, to earn tenure.

In response to the frequent criticism that education professors have forgotten the realities of the classroom, a new staff development plan at Millersville requires education faculty to spend time with pupils in schools. As at the other sites I visited, education faculty were working well into the evening to meet, simultaneously, the requirements for scholarship, excellence in teaching, clinical supervision of education students working in schools, and staying in touch with children and communities.

Learning to Teach Hard-to-Teach Pupils

Another notable feature of the Millersville program is the extent to which it provides its education students with opportunities to learn about the lives and cultures of poor and minority children. The city of Lancaster, only a few miles from the campus, now has a majority of minorities. There is a sizable black population, and an even larger population of migrant and immigrant Hispanics who pluck chickens in local processing plants and harvest fruit. Most are from Puerto Rico. In this way, Lancaster city schools have become a venue for education students' exposure to the challenges of teaching children who are culturally different and usually ill served.

Migrant Education at Millersville

Millersville faculty members in the Migrant Education Program work in the schools attended by the children of migrant workers, providing tutoring and activities meant to enrich these children's experience. The program loans computers to pupils who do not have access to them at home, and Millersville faculty train the pupils as well as their parents to use the computers.

In an attempt to recruit more minority teachers for the Lancaster schools, Millersville at first attempted to offer college courses to black and Hispanic aides working in Lancaster schools, but the union representing the aides objected to the idea that some employees would get time off to take courses, while others would have to work a full schedule. Rather than fight the union, Millersville placed some of the aides in campus jobs and provided them with scholarships.

In the summer of 1991, Millersville faculty, school teachers, and students made a ten-day trip to Puerto Rico, to study the island's culture and schooling, and there are plans to create an exchange program that not only will provide Millersville education students with an immersion experience in Puerto Rico but will also bring Puerto Rican educators and students to the Millersville campus.

The early exposure of education students to Puerto Rican children is designed to chip away at negative attitudes commonly found in the comfortable, isolated, white population of the area. "It's a matter of familiarity and understanding," says Ginny Robbins, director of migrant education at Millersville. Direct, one-to-one contact with these children, and education students' discovery that these children are smart, help inoculate the children against the unsympathetic, ignorant attitudes commonly found among faculty in the schools where Millersville students are placed. Robbins gave me several examples of the attitudes she often encounters in nearby schools:

- During a faculty meeting in an elementary school, the principal exhorted the teachers to raise the level of students' achievement.

"Look at what we have to work with," said a teacher. "These kids can't learn." The principal said, "You're going to have to *learn* how to raise their achievement, because that's who's in the school now."

- One of the teachers visiting schools in Puerto Rico said, "Why don't we get *these* kids in our classes?"
- A teacher assigned a newly arrived Puerto Rican child to a "helper" who did not speak Spanish.
- A teacher said to Robbins, "We're setting these kids up for failure. Lower your expectations!"

Robbins finds that unsympathetic teachers often refer immigrant and migrant kids to special education. When the students remain in regular classes, these teachers tend to seat them in the back of the room and leave them alone.

Preservice teachers are exposed to a simulation of migrant students' experience. They attend a class that is not conducted in their own language. This simulation reflects a growing conviction among educators that there is a strong relationship between feelings and educational change: simply admonishing people to be sympathetic, or lecturing them (in English) on the experience of non-English speakers in North American schools, is not likely to effect change.

Millersville also has a cable hookup with a nearby high school, McCaskey, which not only has a multiethnic student body but also is a member of Ted Sizer's Coalition of Essential Schools. There are permanent camera mounts in the classrooms of teachers who have given the university permission to "tune in" to their classes. When Millersville students have some spare time, they can sit before a large screen and watch McCaskey teachers at work with their students.

Growing Their Own

Millersville is also the site of a Governor's School, a state program to bring talented high school students onto college campuses for a summer exposure to college-level work in their fields of interest. At Millersville, the Governor's School for Teaching recruits academically able high school juniors who are interested in becoming teachers. Outstanding public school teachers are recruited to serve as summer faculty. A special effort to recruit talented minority high school students has paid off. Last year, seven minority students from the previous summer's Governor's School for Teaching enrolled in Millersville as education students.

Students in the summer program needed real children to work with, and many children in the area needed an intensive summer program of academic reinforcement and enrichment. Millersville put the two needs together and designed a summer-school-within-a-school. Forty fifth and sixth graders, a cross-section of kids from the Migrant Education Program, the Lancaster school district, and other local school systems, came to the summer program. Governor's School students get to watch superior teachers in action and get hands-on experience as helpers and tutors.

Out in the Schools

The motif of the education program at Millersville is "the teacher as leader." Faculty leaders anticipate a future when teachers will assert greater authority over curriculum development, policy making, management of resources, and enforcement of professional standards for teaching. The program attempts to prepare students for those leadership roles.

Interviews with student teachers and Millersville graduates who are teaching in local schools suggest that the program is not yet producing teachers who see themselves as leaders. I ran across many more teachers from Millersville than from other sites who believed that the public did not respect them or recognize the complexity of their job. Many commented on the "negative effects" that the union's "militancy" had on public attitudes. The teachers who expressed these views seemed more inclined to retreat into the private satisfactions of teaching than to lock horns with the union, the administration, or the public.

I asked a number of students and former students about what they had found useful or not useful in their training at Millersville, as well as about the rigor of their academic and professional courses. These are some of the things they said:

- A first-year physics teacher said, "I got 'overslammed' with content and didn't have enough protected practice. Much of my student teaching time was spent just sitting in class, watching a teacher put on a show. My science courses emphasized content at the expense of process, and science is as much a process as it is a body of facts."
- An English teacher said, "It is very important to stress content. English teachers need to study grammar because it is the hardest thing to teach."
- A social studies teacher said, "I had good experiences while observing in schools and got to try things out in my junior and senior years. My foundations teacher wasn't effective at all, but, in general, I feel comfortable with my preparation to teach."
- A secondary school teacher said, "I had a jaundiced view of education courses, but I had to come back and take almost fifty credits. I resented having to take so many courses. It would have been great if I could have had an apprenticeship."
- A graduate student with a B.A. in music, now seeking certification as an elementary school teacher, is glad she has a degree in her field, but "no matter how much you know, you still have to know how to represent it to kids. I feel challenged when teaching math, science, and history and wish I had degrees in all those subjects. I took biology and two physics courses, but there is still a lot I don't know. Since it would take an elementary teacher ten years of schooling to learn all that's needed, and since that isn't possible, the only answer is for elementary teachers to know how to research, how to get information. Most of my education courses were challenging. There was lots of reading and writing and a need to use content knowledge creatively. The junior-year methods course, however, was a waste of time."
- A graduate of Millersville with five years of teaching first grade says, "If anything, there should have been more about methods for teaching subject matter to primary-grade children. Understanding children's emotions are the main thing at this age." She thinks that the education of teachers for primary grades should be separated from the training of teachers for the middle grades. "I would have liked more protected practice—it would

have been better to have had fourteen weeks." Even though she is tenured, this teacher could not imagine herself challenging such unprofessional practices as placing a first-year teacher in the worst class. "If the principal can't see it, what good would it do for me to challenge it?" She believes that the public doesn't respect teachers. "They look at that three-month summer break and figure we've got an easy job. If we had year-round school, people would respect us more. It would be better for the kids as well. In the summer, their minds go on vacation."

- "I hate the union," said another student teacher, "because it only promotes what's good for the union. The leaders sometimes lose sight of the children."

- A student teacher in an elementary school says she "might, in the future, take a public stand" on professional issues. "I would be appalled to teach with an abusive teacher." She thinks the union protects teachers too much and, because of that, bad teachers are allowed to remain in the classroom.

- A Millersville graduate who has been teaching first grade for fifteen years thinks that the caliber of student teachers has gone up in recent years. "Millersville is requiring higher grade-point averages and weeding out people who shouldn't teach." She believes that content and pedagogy are equally important, but that teachers do not have to know everything as long as they are honest about what they do not know. "I know a teacher who can't spell. The kids know that she can't spell, and they give her a lot of help with it. The parents know also. She uses it as a way to teach the children that nobody's perfect."

- In a conversation with a group of student teachers, I heard varying opinions. "The academic courses here aren't very well taught," said one. "The professors dump facts on you, especially in geography. But in the ed school, you learn how to use information." Another said that she had learned more about the application of knowledge in most of her education courses, but that in a few "the information was fluffed up."

If there are any conclusions to be drawn from this random, unscientific sampling of teacher opinion, it is that the preparation of good teachers seems to depend on both strong content and good teaching in both academic and education courses. And good teaching, on the academic side, means something more than lectures, assignments, and tests. It requires getting at the philosophical underpinnings of a discipline, and learning how to apply knowledge. On the education side, it means that the methods courses must be highly substantive, and that the pathways to the application of that substance must be clearly marked. But most state certification requirements are based on another set of assumptions: that academic knowledge can be measured in credit hours, that teaching knowledge can be acquired through the proper number of courses bearing the correct titles, that everybody needs about the same number of credits (exceptions are now made for those entering special education, bilingual education, and a few other specialties), and that nothing has to be connected to anything else. A license to teach requires specified dollops of this and that, with few variations according to the unique demands of specific subject areas or age levels.

On the question of whether Millersville-trained teachers would emerge as a more powerful voice in educational decision making, most teachers I interviewed were pessimistic. In that part of the state, tensions between the local National Education Association affiliates and the public are palpable, seeming to pit the union's relentless preoccupation with salary increases against an affluent public's unwillingness to pay more taxes—a refusal justified by the claim that the job is not only easy but part-time. Caught in the crossfire, young teachers seemed to believe that the union had a role to play in maintaining decent salaries. At the same time, however, many expressed the view that the union should be more concerned about professional issues. More often than not, I saw the quiet resignation that characterizes most teachers in the United States, rather than the "empowered" version that Millersville hopes to produce.

Creative Solutions in an Unfriendly Place

The design of the Millersville teacher education program is economical, synergistic, almost artistic. The designers have seized on the common interests of disparate groups and joined them together creatively. For example, migrant children needed summer school. The profession needed to discover and recognize outstanding teachers. The talents of great teachers needed to be used to develop the next generation of teachers. Would-be teachers, as well as great teachers, needed a deeper understanding of the culture of minority children. Would-be teachers needed hands-on experience with children. Solutions to all of these needs were conjoined in the Governor's School for Teaching. As another example, Millersville education students needed to get out of their white, middle-class cocoons. Lancaster children needed tutoring. They also needed to see that people from their own cultural groups could become teachers. Minority teacher aides needed financial help to get teaching credentials. Solutions to all of these needs were fashioned into a program, the Lancaster Partnership. Finally, many professors of arts and sciences needed to improve the quality of their teaching. Their students needed to think about the pedagogy of subject matter while they were studying it, not afterward. Education professors needed to learn more about the details of content-specific pedagogy. These needs were reconciled in the pedagogy seminars. These examples and others, discussed earlier, show that many elements of Millersville's program are both parsimonious and powerful.

There are paradoxes, however. The program tries to equip its future teachers to become leaders outside the classroom as well as in it, but teacher education exists in a larger context. Once in the schools, these teachers seem oppressed by the tension between the community and the schools. They feel the public's lack of respect for their work, and they recoil. Under these conditions, they are not free to be leaders in discussions of the myriad policies and practices that work against the best interests of the children. Neither are they free to push the union in more professional directions.

It is also paradoxical that the pedagogy seminars coexist with the traditionally disdainful attitudes of faculty in the arts and sciences toward teacher education and prospective teachers. The old, thought-stopping mantras—methods courses are a waste of time; students should study "real" science and math, taught by professors in the disciplines—are evident. There is also some evidence that much of the teaching is in the old mode—lectures and tests—and that some faculty are teaching the students they wish they had, rather than the ones they actually do have. Among the arts and sciences faculty I spoke to, I saw little or no awareness of the past decade's research on the craft of teaching, and little awareness that this knowledge might be of value to them in their own teaching and to those who will teach the next generation of Americans. The paradox that pedagogy seminars coexist with hardliners in the arts and sciences shows once again that change occurs unsteadily, with advances and retreats, and creates tensions wherever it is attempted.

7

Research into Practice, Practice into Research

The Michigan State University (MSU) College of Education is a leader in the effort to discover what teachers need to know about their disciplines and how to teach them to students in the schools. Weaving the elements of teacher education into a coherent whole is an uphill struggle against traditional academic divisions and against trade-union values, but MSU is in the forefront of an effort to link the work of researchers, professors, teachers, and teachers-in-training in schools of professional development.

The College of Education at Michigan State University is one of the most prestigious teacher colleges in the United States. MSU's leading scholars are expanding the body of knowledge about the links among knowledge of subject matter, pedagogy, and students. "Pedagogical content knowledge," as it is called, is the knowledge of how to portray a discipline, and topics within a discipline, so that students can make sense of the material, remember it, and apply it. Conventional teacher education still emphasizes generic teaching methods, classroom management, and discipline techniques. At

MSU, however, more than at other universities, teacher education has been construed as the process of learning to teach subject matter.

MSU's College of Education is home base to the Holmes Group, a consortium of ninety-six research universities organized to reform teacher education. Because of its leadership in this reform group, MSU wields national influence over teacher education. In its initial report, *Tomorrow's Teachers* (1986), the Holmes Group called for more "rigor" in teacher education. The report recommended, among other things, that the member institutions abolish the undergraduate degree in education and require all future teachers first to take a subject matter degree and then to engage in professional studies and supervised practice during a fifth year of college. That idea has been embraced by a number of universities and is now official policy in a growing number of states.

Judith Lanier, former dean of the College of Education, heads another influential reform effort, the Michigan Partnership. With public and private funds, the Partnership supports a network of schools of professional development, which are on the cutting edge of an effort to improve clinical training for future teachers and promote collaboration between practitioners and scholars on research and standards of practice.

Important Findings About
Teachers' Content Knowledge

The College of Education is the home of the National Center for Research on Teacher Education led by Mary Kennedy. It has attracted some of the most productive educational researchers in the nation. Some are recognized for their scholarship in the disciplines as well as for their investigations into the details of teaching and learning particular content. Since 1986, studies produced by the center's scholars have reaffirmed the importance of deep and flexible knowledge of subject matter. At the same time, these studies question whether teachers will acquire the necessary depth and flexibility merely by taking more of the existing courses in academic departments.

The center's scholars have documented basic deficiencies in the subject matter knowledge of most teachers, even those with degrees in the subjects they are teaching. Equally important are deficiencies in graduates' conceptual understanding of their fields. They may know the facts of a discipline, but not its underlying principles. They may know the most recent views within a discipline, but not the history of how those views were developed and came to be accepted. They may know what their professors think is true, but nothing about rival views. Even if they know quite a bit about their own specialties, they rarely learn how their disciplines are related to other bodies of knowledge.

All of this may sound unnecessarily "advanced" for people who are merely going to go out and teach children. But children are natural philosophers and frequently ask questions that begin with "Why . . ." or "Who says . . ." or "How do you know . . ." or "What's the purpose of. . . ." They want to know where the periodic table came from, but typical chemistry majors do not know, because they have not studied the history of science. Students want to know what you can do with calculus, but typical math majors cannot say, because they were not expected to apply calculus to anything real. History majors who mastered the "facts" of history but were never exposed to historiography may not know that they have been fed particular interpretations of history, or even that historical interpretation depends on the ideology of the historian or on the preoccupations of a particular generation or nationality. Such teachers lack the *primary tools* for connecting subject matter with the minds of their students.

School children wonder about the world as they find it, not according to the tight categories called disciplines. They ask questions in history that require teachers to know something about science, and vice versa. A college student whose mind is in the deep grooves of a single discipline is poorly equipped to handle the interdisciplinary minds of students.

Still more crucial are the deficiencies in graduates' ability to translate subject matter content for young people who are encountering a subject for the first time. As topics whirl by in a college course, future teachers often are not aware of how they themselves are learning, or not learning. Neither are they thinking about metaphors, examples, explanations, or simulations that they can use to get these topics across to their future students.

Pedagogical content knowledge is a no-man's-land in most universities. Academic faculty members may think a great deal about their own teaching, but they tend to see it as a highly personal, idiosyncratic matter. Few are aware of the systematic inquiries that have been made into the art and science of teaching, and even those who are aware generally do not consider this a worthy branch of knowledge. In most schools of education, the tradition has been to offer future elementary teachers a general methods course. Bits and pieces of content-related teaching knowledge may be part of a course, but much of what I saw (except in mathematics) was thin gruel. Most secondary teachers do take content-specific methods courses; but, here again, much of the material concerns what the teacher does, not what students think or how they arrive at understanding.

These studies documenting what teachers do not know about content and how to teach it have deepened and refined the Holmes Group's understanding of the meaning of "rigor." By 1989, the group had rejected the idea that rigor could be achieved by simply requiring more academic coursework. Instead, it recommended that more challenging content be one part of a transformed education offered to prospective teachers, in which specific subject knowledge would be connected to the whole domain of knowledge, as well as to the many ways in which students might perceive and understand it. The group also noted that the study of subject matter in most universities is designed as a progression toward the particular, whose reward is the Ph.D., not toward an expanding horizon of knowledge.

The very way in which future teachers are taught in the university is a lesson in how not to teach. University professors lecture, assign, give multiple-choice tests, and expect that some students will "get it" and some will not. Teaching, understood as a disciplined and informed effort to reach the minds of students, is not practiced in most university courses.

Dealing with these problems is another matter, however. According to the Holmes Group, teacher educators, even with a compelling case in hand, were not having much luck persuading their colleagues in the arts and sciences to change either their curricula or their teaching methods.

A Shotgun Marriage

On the MSU campus itself, the effort to upgrade subject matter preparation has been extraordinarily difficult. The College of Education's proposal to create a five-year program, requiring, among other things, that future elementary teachers take more advanced mathematics and science courses, was fiercely resisted for years by arts and science faculties, especially those from the departments of mathematics and science.

According to one education professor, there was "an incredible series of the most bitter meetings, with people storming out in tears, and the most astonishing behavior on the part of arts and sciences faculty members." Another professor, however, says that relationships between adversaries have settled down, and that arts and science professors from some departments below the level of high policy are working closely and well.

That the College of Education had so much trouble gaining approval for a longer program of study may be explained in part by its tiny size. There are about 43,000 students on campus, and only 1,000 of them are enrolled in undergraduate teacher education. However nationally distinguished, the College of Education does not appear to have much leverage on campus.

Education faculty members offered other explanations. One professor said that arts and sciences deans "were so fixated on the idea that anything coming out of the ed school is bad, and anything coming out of arts and sciences is good, that they were blind to the plan's advantages." Another claimed that the university faculty feared a drop in enrollment and consequent loss of state funds—aspiring teachers would enroll elsewhere, where they could get a teaching license in four years. Also, said another, academic departments, especially science and math, had used the school of education as a dumping ground for students who did not look like prospective graduate students, and they did not relish the idea of having education students in their upper-division courses.

Whether or not this is true at Michigan State, there is considerable evidence that it is true in many universities. The California State University System, for example, has been trying since 1989 to make the education of teachers a campuswide responsibility on its nineteen campuses. Even with seed money to induce academics to revamp their courses, with sponsorship of interchanges between practicing teachers and academics about what teachers need to know, and with admonitions to academics to encourage bright students to become teachers, "in some disciplines, faculty members have the attitude that if you are not very good, you should become a teacher," says David C. Cohen, chairman of California's system-wide academic senate's teacher education committee.[1] At MSU, despite instances of fraternization across the great divide, it is clear that a real marriage of content and pedagogy will be a long time coming in some disciplines.

According to leaders in the College of Education, Gunther Stahl, an influential science professor, was one of the principal opponents of the plan. In a telephone interview, however, Stahl said he was pleased that future teachers will take more mathematics and science courses, and that he was especially pleased with the plan to increase the math and science requirements for future elementary teachers. Nevertheless, he fears that many of the students will have trouble passing advanced courses.

When I asked him whether the math and science courses would be redesigned to address deficiencies, Stahl at first said that there were no plans to change the curriculum. As to teaching methods in his department, "that's a matter of the individual professor's personality and preference." But he also said that there is a science education unit within the College of Natural Sciences that ensures "coordination" between his department and the College of Education.

Stahl seemed only dimly aware of the accumulating research generated at Michigan State on the teaching of mathematics and science. He mentioned a study, from another university, on why so many students drop out of college science and mathematics programs. This study found that the dropouts believed that their professors did not really "care." "We are working on that," Stahl said.

"Caring," I said, "is not what the cognitive research is about. It's about the way teachers present difficult material so that students actually understand it." I gave Stahl some examples of the glaring knowledge deficiencies of graduates from his own department, turned up by MSU researchers, but Stahl gave the telephone version of a shrug. "It takes some people a long time to absorb those ideas," he said.

"But even little kids are learning the concepts these math majors lack," I said.

"Some do, some don't," he said.

As the conversation went back and forth, I came to understand why Stahl did not seem alarmed by the conceptual failings of graduates of his own department and was not very curious about discoveries in content-specific pedagogy. Stahl thinks that American schools are doing a good job in math and science education. He does not think that international comparisons of student achievement in math and science are valid.

"We are trying to educate everybody," he said, "and the Chinese, Japanese, and Germans are not. We have African-Americans, Hispanics, Pacific Islanders, and, of course, Native Americans."

Given our lack of cultural homogeneity, Stahl believes that the United States is doing as well as can be expected. He urged me to write a "positive" book about teachers, because he thinks that politicians exaggerate American teachers' failings in science and mathematics in order to justify increased funding.

Stahl's viewpoint is very American. Harold Stevenson of Michigan State University, who has spent a decade comparing math education in the United States, China, and Japan, finds that most Americans believe that success in mathematics is a matter of innate ability, while Asians believe that success comes through effort. Stevenson attributes the superior performance of Asian students not only to better teaching but also to cultural beliefs about the importance of effort and persistence. For the American who believes in a genetic explanation, there is no reason to believe that better teaching would significantly improve results.

The gulf between the mentality of the "hard" sciences and the mentality of educators, as revealed at Trinity, Millersville, and Michigan State, poses a serious obstacle to the achievement of national goals for student achievement in those disciplines. Where cooperation exists, it is usually voluntary among individuals on the same campus, who happen to share beliefs about the nature of knowing and understanding and who take the education of future teachers seriously.

The picture of interdepartmental relationships at MSU is a snapshot taken at a particular moment in time. Tensions between education and the academic departments were higher than usual, at least at the governance level, because the battle over the issue of the five-year program had recently occurred. Since that time, the abrasions incurred in the battle have begun to heal, and cooperative relationships are developing between academic and education professors. If there is a lesson in Michigan State's experience, it is that even the most reasonable changes are initially costly but possible nevertheless.

Fighting for the Souls of Twenty-Year-Olds

At MSU, would-be teachers are not accepted into the College of Education until the junior year. Those who intend to teach in elementary schools are required to take TE 101, Exploring Teaching, in the sophomore year, to find out whether they want to become teachers.

I watched a section of TE 101 taught by Tom Bird, a professor of education. In contrast to the passivity I had seen in education students elsewhere, the students in Bird's class were active and engaged, sometimes almost feverish with anxiety. A group of four students taught a lesson in mathematics that they had worked up as a critique of an article on "mathematics learning in context" by a noted MSU professor of mathematics, a leading light in the pedagogy of mathematics. The article was disquieting to most of the students because it challenged their ideas about what a math lesson ought to be like.

There was urgency in the class discussion that followed, and I could hear the clang of cognitive dissonance in the students' comments. Some students thought that the approach took up too much time. One said it was designed to "teach all children," a comment that seemed designed to curry favor with Bird, but clumsily.

Clearly, something unusual was going on in this class. The students were writhing over the ideas, rather than dutifully taking notes or pretending to be awake. Bird did not reward "right" comments or demur on "wrong" ones. He remained stalwartly neutral, throwing the judgment of what was good or bad back to the students and pushing them to justify their beliefs about teaching. If Tom Bird had any preference for one opinion or another, I could not detect it. His studied neutrality seemed to be the source of the students' agitation, because they could not figure out how to please him.

Bird's syllabus and teaching methods, as well as the students' reactions to the course, have been studied by scholars at MSU. The course design rests on well-documented findings in research. First, prospective teachers enter education programs believing that teaching is telling and doing—that the teacher pours information into empty heads, gives tests, grades papers. The trick is in the telling, and education students think they already know how to do that because they have watched so many others do it. Second, these views of entering students directly contradict what most teacher educators now believe: that school children come to school with firmly implanted ideas about how the world works—correct ones, incorrect ones, and incomplete ones—and that these ideas must be known to the teacher before any real progress can be made. There is compelling evidence that a teacher can "tell" until the students turn blue, but unless the learners struggle with the incongruities between what they already think they know and what the teacher wants to impart, no real learning takes place. The teacher's job is to get inside the students' minds and orchestrate their progress toward understanding. Third, and most important, teacher educators have been spectacularly unsuccessful so far in their efforts to change how their students think about teaching and learning.

Bird has designed a course that puts these three pieces of solid evidence together. He pushes his students to bring their unexamined beliefs about teaching to the surface. He shows videotapes of conventional and unconventional teachers at work. He assigns provocative readings. Then he has his students write conversations in which these rival conceptions contend with one another. The writing assignments are stressful because students are expected to contend against their own deeply held opinions and because this conversational form of debate is entirely foreign to most students.

Bird tries to strike the difficult balance between giving students the autonomy to make up their own minds and presenting written and videotaped evidence that makes a compelling case for a radical change in their beliefs. In refusing to be the authority figure who tells his students the "right" way to teach, Bird hopes that his students will resolve the conflicts in their own minds, rather than parrot back what they think he wants to hear.

MSU researchers Linda M. Anderson, Barbara Sullivan, and Steve Swidler studied the impact of Tom Bird's approach to his students.[2] They found, predictably, that the students are driven wild by Bird's lack of response to their comments and presentations, even though he assures them that their standing in class is not affected by his opinions about their comments. And he goes farther: to promote honest expression and free exploration, he does not grade them on class participation. But his students are so accustomed to authoritarian teachers that some have been known to dissolve in tears because they cannot figure out what Bird wants.

Bird does exercise his authority as a grader of the written conversations. When students ignore or misconstrue arguments in the texts that they have read, or when they fail to consider important issues, he writes comments on their papers. Again, however, his students are uncomfortable: they are accustomed to teachers who grade their written work on the basis of definite rules that, if followed will earn them a good grade; they are not accustomed to a teacher who engages their ideas and challenges their logic or interpretations. The researchers found that when students received less than satisfactory grades from Bird, they "complained that Bird was not being clear enough about what they should do to write good papers."

The intellectual burdens of TE 101 are heavy. Students must continually delve into the content of all disciplines. For many, mathematics and science arouse anxiety. The assigned materials are not easy to read, and they contain utterly foreign ideas. Bird says that few have "learned the intellectual moves—reading for meaning, detecting assumptions, comparing the warrants of arguments, and so on—necessary to carry out the task on their own."[3]

The emotional burdens may be even heavier. Students who were cocksure about their ability to teach began to suffer doubts. Students who were used to getting high grades sometimes got low ones and did not understand why. Students who were used to working alone and competing against all others now had to work coop-eratively on complex assignments.

The researchers conclude that teaching for conceptual change, which is what Bird is trying to do, is very hard work. Even if students reconsider their ideas and learn to think for themselves, the power of their own experience as students, the norms in the schools where they will teach, and the reinforcement of their orig-inal notions by parents and friends will probably override the ex-perience of a single course.

The researchers are concerned about the anxieties that the course generates, although Bird himself does not worry that stu-dents will be harmed by their anxiety. Rather, he fears that too much anxiety will cause them to discount his course, in order to preserve their view of "teaching as telling" and their estimation of themselves as competent learners. Nevertheless, the students in Bird's class become much more skilled at constructing arguments and writing about them credibly. That in itself would seem to be a great gift to the students and a blessing for the profession, which is often presumed by its harshest critics to harbor the fuzzy-minded and the barely literate.

Sharing Science and Teaching Knowledge
at Holt High School

Holt High School, within driving distance of MSU, has one thou-sand students, most of them from low-income, blue-collar families, yet the school consistently thrusts up students who win national honors in science competitions. Holt has been designated a Profes-sional Development School in the Michigan Partnership, directed by MSU. Teachers, faculty from MSU, and student teachers collab-orate on improving the mentoring of student teachers and first-year teachers, work together to refine their teaching, and conduct re-search on issues deemed worthy of investigation by all the parties involved. And just as MSU faculty members influence education at Holt, Holt teachers influence teacher education at MSU.

The Holt faculty voted to lengthen every class period by five minutes, so that it could devote every Wednesday morning to col-legial work on teaching and curriculum. Parents were assured that their children would not miss a minute of instruction, even though the students do not come to school until 11:00 A.M. on Wednesdays.

In a Wednesday morning meeting of the science faculty, Randy, a doctoral student with some years of teaching experience, presented a case study of a lesson he had taught as a first-year teacher. The class was a general science course for students at the low end of the academic scale. Randy had tried to get his students to take some responsibility for their own learning, but the effort had not gone well.

Randy described a class session in which he set up an experiment with marshmallows and a microwave oven, to explore the kids' ability to apply what they had learned. The students did observe that marshmallows expanded in the oven, but there were differences of opinion about whether the air or the water in the marshmallows explained the expansion. Randy then tried to model the approach that real scientists use to settle disputes: he created additional experiments designed to take the students' thinking a bit farther. When that did not produce consensus, he asked the students to design their own experiments.

Despite evidence refuting the "air" theory, some students clung to that belief. One student said that she really believed in the "air" theory but did not want to say so when the group had changed to the "water" theory. Another "air" theorist claimed that he had never believed in the "air" theory at all. In the class discussion, nobody made any reference to anyone else's experiment. According to Randy, there was no evidence that the students had transferred this knowledge to anything else. They "played with the microwaves for a while," he said, "and were then ready to go on to something else."

The experienced teachers in the meeting reacted to Randy's presentation.

"Sophomores, in my experience, don't relate to each other's work until the end of the term," said one.

"Students at all levels avoid designing experiments which refute their hypotheses," said another.

Yet another teacher observed that the kids had been conditioned to be passive, especially the special-education kids in the class: "At-risk kids are often rigid and don't listen to others, just like preschool kids."

In the same vein, still another teacher commented that the kids had rarely been in classes where the knowledge they generated was taken seriously and was incorporated into the knowledge of the class.

Commenting on the student who had denied changing his mind, a researcher said that people often deny changing their minds, and that most are unwilling to admit being wrong. "Most people cannot track their own thoughts over time," he said.

An experienced teacher of physics noted that change is emotional, not logical: "*Something* has to happen earlier in life so that students find the joy in doing their own experiments and changing as a result of the experiment."

Obstacles to Professionalism: Unions, Administrators, and Academics

Creating the kind of scene just described, where teachers learn from each other, has not been easy. According to Andy Anderson, a science specialist in the College of Education, "There were long and difficult negotiations. Some departments were resistant to the idea of a Professional Development School, and we had to decide whether to have only some departments involved and not others. The union at Holt dragged its feet, but ultimately it listened to its members. If the faculty wanted something, the union didn't put up roadblocks."

As MSU built its network of Professional Development Schools, there were battles with administrators over the selection of mentors. Some principals were used to picking the faculty harridan, or to passing out the "plum" of a mentorship as they saw fit, or to assigning student teachers to the weakest teachers.

Anderson regrets the lack of systematic cooperation between MSU science faculty and the College of Education. "Very few students come to be science teachers by way of the science department," he says. "The mentality of many science professors is weeding out, rather than teaching. The science faculty is a subgroup that doesn't know how to evaluate what students have learned. They know nothing about either evaluation or pedagogy. The problem is just ignorance." Anderson is nevertheless optimistic about the future. "Individual science faculty members are willing to orient their curriculum and teaching toward the needs of future science teachers. The few who ask themselves whether their students are really learning are the ones who are beginning to change."

Anderson also notes the common belief among academic faculty that teachers learn to teach by teaching, and not through the study of pedagogy. This belief is faulty, he says. "Teachers are so isolated that they don't have any way to validate what they do, or to know whether what they did worked or not. Teaching is an oral tradition, not a written tradition."

The Professional Development School experiment at Holt is bearing fruit. Holt teachers have been able to describe how their practice has changed as a result of their interactions with one another. The mentor teachers have changed teacher education at MSU "enormously," says Anderson, making it more practical. Most important, the student body, against all odds, is making a name for itself in American education.

8

What Is Ideal
in Teacher Education?

Under the right conditions, ordinary people with a reasonably strong academic record in high school, a sincere desire to teach, and a faint interest in the life of the mind can be turned into strong beginning teachers who are broadly educated and who have lively, inquiring minds and the moral conviction required for teaching in today's schools.

Idealized portraits of teacher education abound. The authors of these portraits have made lists of things that education students should know and be able to do, have prescribed the credit hours that they should take in various departments and subjects, and nearly always have advocated more emphasis on academic subjects and practice in the schools and less time in education courses. From Myron Lieberman (1956)[1] to James B. Conant (1963)[2] and James D. Koerner (1965)[3] to John Goodlad (1990),[4] analysis of the deficiencies in teacher education has not changed very much. These authors' prescriptions for change differ only slightly, reflecting the temper of the decade in which each one wrote and whatever brand of educational craziness was afflicting the schools at the time. Some of their recommendations are finally being heeded; others are not.

Instead of another detailed list of reforms, this chapter presents a small list of ideas about what goes into the making of a highly accomplished beginning teacher. The ideas are drawn from observations of great teachers in their early years of teaching and from interviews with them in which I sought evidence of any connections between the qualities and skills they brought to their classrooms and the schools of education that had trained them. My judgments about which teachers were good were not tied to any supposedly objective criteria, such as test scores of the students they taught.

The outstanding beginning teachers emerged from all kinds of programs—four-year, five-year, and postbaccalaureate fifth-year programs. Some came from schools that emphasized subject matter more than is typically the case; some came from more traditional programs. Since good teachers can come from bad programs, and vice versa, I plied these better-than-average beginners with questions that sought connections that went beyond happenstance, for patterns in their various training programs that seemed to account for their intellectual liveliness, their self-confidence, and their ability to focus on the students rather than on themselves.

Some patterns emerged. The better-than-average schools of education screen out those who do not have respectable SAT or ACT scores, or who are not at least C-plus or B-minus performers in their freshman and sophomore academic courses. Good schools of education find systematic ways to discourage aimless, immature, or unthinking students.

Good schools of education also work hard to create coherence—within and among the academic, professional, and clinical components of a student's education. Faculty members who are striving for coherence are not easily discouraged by contemptuous academics or sulky union leaders. They tend to be happy warriors.

Good education faculties organize opportunities for their students to construct their own versions of coherence, requiring them to talk, debate, and write about serious issues and intractable problems in teaching. They afflict their students with disquieting ideas, but they also comfort them when they are overwhelmed by a bad day in the classroom. Faculty members are uninhibited about dealing with the moral and ethical dimensions of teaching and have the language essential to the discussion of those dimensions.

Beginning teachers seem much more prepared for the rigors of teaching when their schools of education arrange rapid alternation between formal study and practice in the schools. The process of learning to teach seems to be accelerated if students are made to interpret events in the classroom soon after they have experienced them, if they are given the chance to see manifestations of theories soon after studying them, and if they get quick and honest feedback on all aspects of their work.

In good schools of education, professors invest much time and energy in the development of training sites for their student teachers or interns. They sneak around the school district's power structure to discover, select, and train excellent cooperating teachers and mentors. They recognize that good teachers know things that professors do not. Most important, they are willing to play the sometimes unpleasant role of gatekeeper to the profession.

I found that where these conditions existed it was the school of education, not the school of arts and sciences, that was turning an otherwise passive group of students (or, at least, most of them) into intellectually alive, confident, self-critical teachers. In light of these observations, I offer the following suggestions.

Raise and Enforce College Admission Standards

A truly reformed system of teacher education would begin with elevated and enforced admission criteria for entering freshmen. Beginning college students must be able to read well, write clearly, and perform mathematical operations beyond the level of arithmetic.

But publicly supported colleges and universities receive state funds on the basis of enrollment. They have little incentive to screen out those who are unable to do college-level work. The laxness of college entrance standards shows up more and more in the high failure rate of college sophomores and juniors who apply for admission to schools of education and cannot pass preadmission tests of basic literacy. Not only have these low-scoring students been admitted to college, they have "passed" freshman and sophomore courses in English and mathematics without making noticeable progress in reading, writing, and mathematics. That so many college students cannot qualify for the tougher standards of selective schools of education substantiates the claims of the teacher educators I interviewed: arts and sciences professors who teach lower-division courses do not know very much about their students' reading ability, because they spend so little of their class time in class discussions where they might discover that students have not understood their reading assignments. Neither do they detect deficiencies in students' writing abilities, because they so rarely ask their students to write. Higher admission and teaching standards would improve the intellectual climate for all students, whether they plan to become teachers or not.

There is a hitch, though. Higher admission standards, consistently applied, screen out disproportionate numbers of minority students who want to be teachers but whose previous education has not prepared them to do college-level work. G. Pritchy Smith of the University of North Florida has documented about 90,000 minority students who wanted to teach but were either kept out of education programs or denied licenses on the basis of test scores. The low scores, Smith says, reflect "the poor quality of K–12 education for poor and minority students . . . in almost every school district in the nation."[5]

We need these people who are longing to be teachers, and we need them in classrooms now. They bring to schools the heart and deep commitment that are just as critical to the education of poor and minority students as academic competence is. We cannot wait until citizens in affluent school districts are willing to pay for better schools in poor school districts. That may not happen for generations. We can try to stop the failure cycle now, by insisting that publicly supported colleges help otherwise promising minority students meet the academic standards for education schools, and by insisting that states give the universities the money to do the job right. As Goodlad points out, colleges and universities do not think twice about remedial programs for athletes. Why not have such programs for future teachers? Money spent on their education surely has more power to benefit the general welfare than money spent to keep athletic stars in college.

Insist on a Sound, Coherent Liberal Arts Program

Nearly everybody agrees that a good "liberal arts" education and "depth" in subject matter are necessary prerequisites for good teaching. The virtues of a rich liberal arts education are so tirelessly touted in speeches by university chancellors, presidents, and provosts that it begins to seem as if this lofty ideal were being held up by rhetoric alone. The reality of liberal arts education, as countless critics have noted and documented, is quite degraded. A few universities have defined a "common core" of liberal learning and worked hard to ensure a balanced, coherent education for undergraduates, but they are very few. On most campuses, "the liberal arts" has come to mean an environment where professors can teach almost anything they like and students can take almost any courses they wish, as long as they have brushed by a few basic survey courses. Citizens do not seem to care whether future engineers, businessmen, or dentists know anything about history, philosophy, political science, or literature. They do care whether future teachers are generally and broadly educated—and they should care. For teachers, a wider understanding of the great branches of learning is not merely something that is nice to have, a lower-middle-class version of finishing school; it is the warp and weft of their work as teachers.

If Americans want their teachers to be well-educated people, then they will have to insist that public colleges and universities organize coherent, thoughtfully taught undergraduate liberal arts programs that include a lot of writing. The need is especially acute in the case of those who plan to teach all subjects in elementary or middle schools. The Interdisciplinary Studies Program at the University of Texas at San Antonio (see Chapter Three) provides one outstanding example of how this might be accomplished. Not only do future elementary teachers study all the requisite academic disciplines, they do so in ways that help them see connections and relationships among disciplines.

The colleges have dithered on this issue for decades. Universities have kept legislatures at bay by shamelessly invoking the principle of academic freedom. They have kept accrediting associations at bay with sweetly stated intentions ("We have just formed a committee and are taking a look at that"). They have kept teacher educators at bay through budgetary and psychological intimidation. They have kept the public at bay by shifting the blame for teachers' deficiencies in subject matter knowledge to schools of education. This last tactic is especially threadbare. For many decades, secondary teachers in the United States have completed the same general and major requirements as those imposed on nonteachers. If they are not broadly educated and do not know their subject matter deeply enought to teach it well, it is the fault of arts and sciences departments in universities.

Insist on the Integration
of Liberal and Professional Studies

In an ideal education program, students taking courses in math, history, or science would simultaneously be thinking about the pedagogical implications of what they were learning. Such integration seldom occurs, however; the traditional sequence of courses usually separates content and pedagogy in time, and the wall between arts and sciences and schools of education has become almost impenetrable. That wall is more permeable in small liberal arts colleges with education programs, but the tendency to separate content from teaching knowledge is still evident.

In the pedagogy seminars at Millersville University (see Chapter Six), students in an academic course meet with the course professor and a professor from the school of education. The students become students of their own learning, as well as students of the professor's teaching. They begin to think about what it takes to get ideas and concepts across to people who do not already know them. The beauty of this model is that everybody benefits. The students discover how to learn better; they begin to think as teachers must think. The education professor deepens his or her knowledge of how subject matter and pedagogy intersect. The academic professor gets detailed feedback on his or her teaching.

Achieving this economical and elegant integration of content and pedagogy is not easy. But if the Millersville model, or models that address the same need, were to become a normal part of teacher education, a lot of the time now consumed by methods courses could probably be compressed into fewer class hours, which would leave more time for students to work in schools—as observers, practice teachers, or interns.

Send Would-Be Teachers Out to the Schools Early

Lots of students enter college with the dream of becoming teachers. Most of them, it appears, think they already know how to teach, although their ideas about teaching are apt to be naïve and incomplete. Good schools of education actively disabuse these students of their innocent ideas in the freshman or sophomore year, by sending them out into the schools for a dose of reality and by requiring them to take tough introductory courses.

This early exposure to the hard world of teaching not only sifts out those who are not cut out for it but also prods students along the path to adulthood. Few other college students have the same real-world experiences before graduation, and few have to take real risks and face the consequences. Students in good teacher education programs do.

Wring the Water Out of the Education Courses

I saw little evidence of teacher education "bloat" in my visits to six campuses, but there is plenty of scholarly and anecdotal evidence for a lot of redundancy within and among the courses that future teachers are required to take. The same topic, worthy though it may be, appears in the introductory education course, the educational psychology course, and the general course on teaching methods. As one recent graduate told me, "There is only one course, and it's taught over and over again."

NCATE tries to get at this problem by forcing its members to articulate a coherent theme for the overall program of professional studies and to justify the design of particular courses in relation to that theme. But NCATE's process is still being invented. Even if it were highly adept at sniffing out needless duplication, the fact remains that the tenure system makes it hard for deans of schools of education to reeducate or get rid of people who make a living through redundancy. Moreover, the majority of education schools still do not belong to NCATE.

For decades, teachers have criticized the needless duplication in their education courses. They have expressed their annoyance with all the courses that merely taught them complicated words for ordinary things. To the extent that teacher educators have failed to respond to these criticisms, they have made themselves vulnerable to external attack. Legislatures have mandated fewer courses. Provosts have pulled the purse strings tighter. Arts and sciences professors have been handed another log to pile on the fires of their everlasting contempt. The price for more generous public support of teacher education may be evidence that schools of education are listening to justifiable criticisms and willing to take appropriate action.

Teach Teachers the Things Best Learned on a Campus

The notions that teaching can be learned only on the job and that all education courses are a waste of time negate education itself. The purpose of formal study is to give students a systematic, critical exposure to a field of inquiry, help them know what is known (as well as recognize what is not known), and enable them to imagine possibilities that they can spend a lifetime discovering on their own.

Properly taught, a college course is a more efficient than haphazard way for students to learn how to interpret raw experience, to detect hidden assumptions, and tell the difference between ideology and theory. For example, what assumptions underlie the practice of tracking students according to ability? What theory of human motivation results in state's policy of denying a driver's license to a dropout under the age of eighteen? Is there an implicit ideology in whole-class teaching, or in whole-language instruction, or in cooperative learning?

Systematic instruction in a college course can compel the student to reconcile competing and conflicting views about teaching. Mary Kennedy of Michigan State University says teachers often simultaneously believe that all students should be treated alike and that all students should be treated as individuals. Teachers who have been carefully educated will become aware that the two beliefs are inherently contradictory. As they observe teachers and practice teaching themselves, they learn to spot instances in which this unexamined contradiction plays out to the disadvantage of students. As a consequence, carefully educated teachers will not be shooting quivers of mixed messages at their students.

Intellectually challenging education courses make teachers into thoughtful skeptics. American teachers need to be more skeptical of the "new" teaching methods and models that march through American education in endless ranks of acronyms. They need to know the sad history of failed fads, and they need to recognize them when they reappear under new banners. Good education courses should arouse students' interest in educational research but should also make them wary when they hear a researcher or administrator say, "We now know. . . ." Teachers should be taught to be dubious of what their elders and betters call "settled knowledge."

An example of the short shelf-life of "settled" propositions can be found in a 1980 book by a revered teacher educator. The author takes a middle-ground position on the value of educational research. While acknowledging that most of it is technically flawed and produces no definitive conclusions, he also argues that some "law-like" statements derived from statistical correlations seem to be effective in practice, even if we do not know why these statements are true, and even if the "law-like" statements do not work in absolutely all cases. He gives an example:

> Statistically significant correlations between variables of teacher behavior and those of student behavior or achievement are well established. In practical terms, these correlations yield prescriptions for use in practical settings. For example, if a teacher plies low achieving students with low order questions, provides corrective feedback, assigns work, and holds the students accountable, they will do well on a standard test in the subject. This principle yields a prescription: ask low order questions, give frequent feedback, make assignments, and hold students accountable.[6]

Having accepted the validity of this way of teaching low-achieving students, the author goes on to say that all propositions are qualified. He adds the only qualifications that seemed relevant in 1980:

"The student must be able to read the text; there must be order in the classroom; and there must be sufficient time as well as other conditions."

What this author did not foresee in 1980 was that his "law-like" proposition would be eaten raw by state and local superintendents who were hungry for a research-based approach to "accountability." Curricula, textbooks, and tests were designed around that proposition, and teachers were directed to teach accordingly. Few administrators questioned the value of the tests that the researchers had used to establish this proposition. The law-like statement was soon transformed into a farce, American style, by bureaucratic overkill.

The new version of "We now know . . ." is that low-achieving students, like all others, need both easy work and hard work, the big picture as well as the little steps. It became clear that students who scored well on tests might not be learning much except how to take tests. It also became clear that people who believed that low-achieving students would never amount to much saw in this proposition a justification for expecting little academic progress and for retreating into the vacuous promotion of self-esteem. Now, only thirteen years later, that "settled" piece of knowledge is not so settled after all. An entirely new set of questions has emerged, along with an entirely new set of "research-based propositions."

In this lengthy example, we can see that teachers need systematic education in matters that will never be treated in courses on subject matter. Where will they learn how everything in education affects everything else? Where will they learn to anticipate the sometimes toxic interactions among teaching ideas (such as "law-like" propositions), school politics (such as premature embrace of such propositions by appointed and elected bosses), and economics (such as publishers' designing of "dumbed down" textbooks to sell to administrators who want low-order questions for lower-order people)? This kind of knowledge is necessary for teachers to "speak truth to power" confidently when the powers are about to turn half-truths into bad programs.

Teachers do not learn about such matters on the job, nor do they learn about them in college courses that train them to read unreadable research papers (it would be better to train the researchers to write). They do not learn about them in education courses that indoctrinate them into the latest versions of "settled" knowledge. The kind of skepticism and capacity for systemic analysis that teachers need can be cultivated only in well-designed, intensely practical college courses that are interwoven with experiences in schools.

The Case for Reformed Courses
in Educational Foundations

The systematic study of the "foundations" of education—the history, psychology, sociology, and politics of education—is the logical vehicle for making future teachers aware of the complex forces bearing on the schools. Untutored experience in the public schools is no substitute for formal inquiry, fortified by structured observation in varied school settings and followed up by tough analytical assignments.

As matters stand, foundations courses are anathema to most education students. When we hear teachers complain that teacher education is "too theoretical," it is usually the foundations courses that they are complaining about. And they are right to complain. In most cases, the professors who teach the history, philosophy, sociology, politics, and economics of education are borrowed from academic departments. In their home departments, rigor is defined as the memorization and reproduction of a body of factual knowledge, imparted by lecture and not connected to reality. The connections between this body of knowledge and teaching work are weak, and so the material seems impractical to students.

Nothing could be more practical, however, than a deep understanding of the forces that impinge on a teacher's work. The footprints of philosophy, history, sociology, politics, and economics are all over every curriculum guide, teacher manual, textbook, administrative handbook, union contract, central office memorandum, faculty meeting, and community dispute. Yet many academically oriented professors are so removed from the schools that they cannot see or help their students see these footprints, and few use them as entry points to the more academic exposition of their disciplines.

Foundations courses organized around teachers' experiences, case studies, and analyses of the artifacts of schooling, and taught by persons who know whereof they speak, would be enormously empowering to future teachers. But scholars have not always seen it that way. In 1956, Koerner argued that foundations courses derived from the academic disciplines "should be taught only by persons fully qualified to teach in the appropriate academic departments at the same institution." He went on to say, "If future teachers cannot be guided in these subjects by competent scholars, they would be better off with no formal work at all."[7]

I would argue that "fully qualified" and "competent" scholars are the ones who know their disciplines deeply enough to make the content relevant to professional preparation. Foundations courses that are practical present a greater intellectual challenge than courses that merely call for the recitation of forgettable facts. If those who teach such courses cannot or will not move in a practical direction, then perhaps they should return to their home departments, with our blessing, and let thoughtful teacher educators and practicing teachers do the job.

The Case for Campus Classes in Behavior Management

On the face of it, it would seem that learning how to run a classroom and maintain student discipline should be learned on the job. The evidence shows otherwise, however. There is a codified body of knowledge about classroom and behavior management that provides future teachers not only with a bag of procedures and tricks (which they might learn on the job through mimicry or trial and error) but also with the underlying principles that make the procedures and tricks effective when used appropriately, judiciously, and ethically. The line between discipline and tyranny is not always easy to discern, nor is the line between motivation and manipulation. Future teachers need to talk about theories and principles and practice the techniques derived from them. When practice teachers or interns have learned this body of knowledge, they look like twenty-year veterans rather than awkward beginners.

High-culture mavens often look down on this body of

knowledge, but they should not. Teachers who know how to keep order are free to concentrate on teaching Melville or subtraction or the U.S. Constitution because they are not engulfed in a desperate struggle to keep students under control.

The Case for Formal Studies of Testing and Assessment

Few schools of education teach their students much about testing and assessment. Faculty members usually justify this lapse with the claims that there is not enough time and that psychometrics is too arduous and technical a subject for undergraduates. Perhaps that is true, but teachers can be trained in "philosmetrics"—the study of the assumptions that underlie the construction of standardized, short-answer tests and alternative methods of assessment. They can be trained in "politometrics"—the study of how the testing industry and the educational hierarchy have collaborated in efforts to answer the public's concern about accountability, and to what effect. They can be trained in "bibliometrics"—the study of the grammatical (and ungrammatical), syntactical, and lexical conventions of test-item writers. They can be trained to extract useful information from tests, to write meaningful tests of their own, and to grade tests fairly. They can learn how to prepare their students to do well on tests, without cheating or violating sound educational principles. And they can learn enough basic statistics to hold their own against the intimidating priesthood of psychometricians. Most important, future teachers need to study the various forms of assessment that will replace the current (and ineffective) short-answer tests. Grading of essays, evaluation of portfolios, and construction of demonstrations of mastery should be part of the curriculum for teachers.

Such understanding cannot be acquired on the job or through brief in-service courses. Experienced teachers are seldom able to help beginners, and administrators are sworn by oaths of self-interest to uphold the validity and political significance of tests, whatever kind they may be. Unless teachers learn about testing and assessment in college, they will continue to be victims of tests rather than active collaborators in the necessary effort to find better ways of teaching, learning, and being accountable to the public.

Studying Community As Well As Pedagogy

In 1980, B. Othanel Smith wrote that "the community is not the close intimate web of human associations that we often read about in literature and that many now living experienced in their youth. In little more than a generation this mode of social existence has fallen by the wayside. In its place has evolved a conglomerate of social groups, corporate associations, and organized interests all loosely interdependent and held together partly by some sense of fair play and partly by antagonistic cooperation. . . . Community as a meeting of the minds these days tends to be a recurring event rather than a constant state of affairs."[8]

What was true in 1980 is even more true today. Communities get into battles over the values embedded in curricula, textbooks, disciplinary policies, tests, grouping practices, and budget priorities. School board elections tend to amplify these disputes. Teachers whose training has taken place only in classrooms are woefully unprepared to cope with these regularly occurring eruptions. Some teachers become emotionally devastated. Others try to negate values questions by asserting their technical expertise, which usually makes things worse. Most run for cover, dismissing controversies as "political"—as if they themselves were not employees of a political institution and citizens of a political democracy.

Few schools of education prepare their students to navigate intelligently among contending values. Discussions of values are not the academy's strong suit, and foundations courses touch on these matters only lightly, if at all, or intellectualize them out of existence. That should change. Teachers should be intellectually and emotionally prepared to participate wisely in community discussions of basic values in teaching, learning, and educational policy. Teacher education should include at least a brief study of contemporary American communities, the reading of notable case studies, and opportunities to interview teachers and community members who have endured and resolved community disputes.

Prospective teachers also need to study what goes on in the juvenile justice system, as well as in drug rehabilitation centers, recreation departments, clinics, and churches. Teacher education students at Portland State University (see Chapter Five) were placed in community agencies, to seek their advice for teachers. This is a great example of educating teachers about community.

Change Criteria for Tenure and Promotion
to Reward Good Teaching

What has been said many times before bears repeating: the disproportionate emphasis on published research as the basis for decisions about tenure and promotion is harmful to teaching, especially at the undergraduate level. The desperate pursuit of publication credits by professors with mortgages to pay and children to raise has corrupted university research in the United States and forced academics to overstate its value to society. Worse, it has quietly sanctioned mediocre teaching.

Great teacher educators should model good teaching so that their students will not only hear about it but also experience it. Good teachers do exquisite planning, pay close attention to their students' responses, assign and react to written work, and work with individual students. All of that takes more time than reading from yesteryear's lecture notes, giving multiple-choice tests, and keeping office hours from 2:00 to 3:00 on Tuesdays and Fridays.

Great teacher educators jump into cars and spend time on the road getting to school sites, where they observe and coach their students, work with and learn from teachers, and work directly with children. They read the technical literature in their field, the mountains of teaching materials produced annually in their specialties, and the literature that is the basis of intellectual discourse in many fields.

In addition, teacher educators must "do research" because they are bound by the tenure criteria for professors in academic departments, who do not really have to do any of the time-consuming things that trainers of teachers must do. Previous chapters showed examples of education professors who were straddling the competing demands of academia and the careful preparation of teachers by working twelve-hour days. An entire institution cannot be run on the assumption that professors will or should live such lives. Most teacher educators do not. Either their teaching is not exemplary, because they are driven to produce research, or their research is third-rate, because they spend their time being good teachers and clinical professors.

Changing the tenure criteria in academic departments seems to be too hopeless a goal for the moment, but changing the tenure criteria for professors of education is not out of the question. Professors in other professional schools are not subject to the publish-or-perish rule. They can and do conduct research and publish, but they are not required to; teacher educators should not be required to, either. If tenure criteria can be modified to reflect the realities of a medical, dental, nursing, or law professor's work and primary mission, then they can be modified for those who are teachers of teachers. Since teaching itself, apart from the subject being taught, is one of the most powerful means of influencing the next generation of teachers, great teaching and outstanding clinical work should be the primary means by which professors of education attain tenure and promotion.

Insist on Both Ethical and Academic Qualifications

Many students in today's schools of education seem to be coming out of a time warp. The passive, rigid, xenophobic young ladies who want a socially respectable career, or whose parents may have insisted that they "major in something practical," are still with us in 1992. What they and their parents do not know is that their images of classroom and school life are out of date. In increasing numbers of communities, teaching is more like being a Peace Corps volunteer than being a modern-day version of "Our Miss Brooks."

Teaching work requires flexibility, not rigidity. Merely to hold their ground against the antieducational forces all around, today's teachers need to be tactfully assertive, not passive. It requires a well-developed self to understand and sometimes stare down the brazenly disrespectful students found nearly everywhere today, and to retain a sense of humor and detachment. It takes a real grown-up, not somebody's aimless or sheltered daughter or son, to see the good in all students and call forth their idealism and effort.

Teaching in 1992 requires a person who genuinely enjoys and seeks to learn from the multicultural mix that the United States has become. To lack those qualities is to conspire in the failure of the schools to teach children who are not white and not middle class. Even the smartest, best-trained teachers will not succeed without an authentic belief that all students can learn, and a spirited willingness to learn about their students.

Michelle Wallace, an African-American professor and writer, has said that "the educational system, which doesn't take seriously their [African-Americans'] educational potential, especially as writers, sabotages them from kindergarten to college. Since the Civil Rights Revolution, even more so. Either what they have to learn turns them off, or they're turned off by the spirit in which it is offered."[9]

In very large numbers, risk-avoiding graduates of teaching colleges take no teaching jobs at all rather than jobs where conditions vary from "Leave It to Beaver" expectations. Even if they find teaching jobs in predominantly white, middle-class towns or suburban enclaves, they are probably not the right kind of people to be teaching even those students, who will need to become more flexible and more knowledgeable about the peoples of the whole world if they are to prosper in a polyglot democracy and a global economy.

The reform movement's emphasis on raising the intellectual qualifications of future teachers is warranted. There is a smarter group of people coming into teacher education—but academic smarts are not enough. In many places, the training of teachers is more expert—but technical expertise is not enough. The teachers in today's schools need to be street-smart, courageous, and grounded in the moral ideals of the American experiment. If they are not, then they probably should not be allowed to graduate from schools of education.

Insist on State Funding for Public Schools That Train Teachers

It is easy to be in favor of on-the-job training for teachers. In the case of teachers, however, not just any job or trainer will do. Bad experiences and poor exemplars obliterate even the best preservice training. Only a small number of public schools have begun to see themselves as part of the apparatus for teacher education. Few principals or teachers know what to do about trainees and interns, and there is usually no money to jump-start serious programs. All the old traditions work against a professional approach to school-based teacher education.

Doing the job right will require, at the very least, start-up funds. Because the training of beginners is such a foreign idea in most schools, funding may need to be sustained for a decade or more, until the profession internalizes new norms and develops new traditions. To rely on the passing fancies of corporate or foundation grants, or on the ever-churning priorities of local school boards, or on the rising and falling fortunes of local governments, is to admit that we are not serious about on-the-job training.

In 1963, Conant argued that states should take financial responsibility for practice teaching "to insure high-quality practice teaching as part of the preparation of teachers enrolled in either private or public institutions."[10] He was right then, and he is even more right now. But in all the years since, only a handful of states have made the commitment to this relatively inexpensive, potentially powerful way of improving the education of American teachers. All who want better teachers, especially those who think that teaching people to teach on college campuses is a waste of time, owe it to themselves and to society to vigorously support state funding for the training and induction of teachers.

Part Two

Obstacles to Reform

9

Working Conditions
for American Teachers

One of the most formidable obstacles to improving the quality of the people entering the teaching force is the steady deterioration of the work environment. The good-natured accommodation of so many teachers to disrespectful, alienating conditions should not obscure the fact that the environment in most schools is driving the best of the current generation out of the classroom and into other lines of work.

If, by some miracle, teacher education in the United States became the envy of the developed world, there would remain the problem that self-respecting, intelligent people avoid teaching because the working conditions are deplorable. The usually cited problems—low pay, large classes, lack of supplies, autocratic principals, lack of administrative support, no telephones, no quiet place to work—have been recited so often that we are numbed by the litany.

To those old complaints are added new ones, born of the social crises of our time. For example, many schools are not safe for either students or teachers. And although teachers have always been encumbered by mundane chores, today's mundane chores—patrolling the bathrooms to prevent drug deals, filling out the biography section of each child's federal form because kids can't be trusted to know their own ethnic groups—are more galling than yesterday's (chopping wood and stoking the stove).

Two Class-Size Dramas

Teachers have always thought that they could do a better job with smaller classes, but the complaints about class size have intensified in recent years as teachers try to cope with a larger number of mainstreamed special-education students, as well as with students who are simply needier by virtue of having less contact with adults. Whenever the subject of class size comes up, Washington policy makers, researchers employed by educational bureaucracies, and tax-resisting nabobs of all stripes stage a little opera well known to observers of American education. In the first act, the Duke of Data intones the words of a great Oracle from the olden days (twenty years ago): *small* reductions in class size do not make any difference in students' scores on standardized tests; a chorus chants statistics in the background. In the second act, an element of conflict is introduced. The Prince of Manipulation remembers something else the Oracle said: *large* reductions in class size (down to fifteen, I think the script says) *do* make a difference. Three Knights agonize about what to do. The first one suggests reducing class size for the first grade. The second one proposes small classes for the first three grades. The third one says that would not be fair—teachers in junior and senior high schools need small classes, too. In the third act, with palms upraised, a chorus of richly attired Bravos sorrowfully conclude that there is not enough money in the free world to fund *that* kind of class-size reduction. *Exeunt omnes.*

Another kind of class-size drama is a one-woman, one-act improvisational play staged on a parking lot covered with crushed glass against a backdrop of withered trees. Here, Sarah Mosle, a journalist who spent a year teaching thirty-two children at New York's P.S. 98, gives her interpretation of this play:

> It was nearly impossible to offer individual attention.
> At no point was this more evident than during the first

few moments of class. As you'd walk in, you'd give your kids until you counted five to get their bookbags unpacked, their workbooks out, and their pencils ready: *One.* Natoya is scowling and in tears, for the third time this week. Sixto is trapped in his parka. Could I help him unzip it? *Two.* Yadira is at your waist. She is tiny, like a little angel. She's been to the doctor. You want to listen, but you also want her to sit down. ("I like the way Johary is ready. I like the way Julia is ready.") *Three.* José U.—José U. because you have three Josés in your class—is handing you his math homework. No, you don't want this now. ("Maggie is ready. Arleni is ready.") What happened to all your colored chalk? *Four.* You're wrestling a billowing bedspread of chart paper to the ground. The math coordinator pokes her head in. No, you haven't given the math test yet. ("Michael, let's get going. José C, José W.—*all* Josés—sit down!) Suddenly there's a commotion in the corner. You march up, hands on hips: "What's going on here?" Oh my God. Yamile has just swallowed a button.[1]

It seems that there is also not enough money in the free world to fund a contemporary study of the class-size issue, a study that would measure outcomes with more refined instruments and would take account of what we all know to be true: teachers must form bonds of love and respect with their students in order to get them to care about schoolwork. Those who send their children to private schools with small classes know this very well.

Danger and Sadness

Although teaching in poor and immigrant neighborhoods has always been hard duty, the drugs-plus-guns epidemic of the past few years has increased the hazards of teaching, not only in central cities but also in nearly every highly populated part of the nation. Even where schools take stringent measures to protect teachers and students from assault, the very measures taken to ensure safety also wreak havoc on teachers' working conditions. Many teachers must leave their schools by 3:30 P.M. when the barricades to interior hallways are locked for the night. The vice principals who roam the corridors, like cops on the beat with sizzling walkie-talkies, seem obsessed with order and control, not with teaching and learning. Life in urban schools may be relatively secure during working hours, but many teachers and students are terrified of the trip to and from school.

Moreover, fewer young teachers in this generation seem to be able to tolerate the risks connected with teaching in the cities, or to endure the sadness of their students' lives. One young woman who teaches in a barrio elementary school told me, "I don't know how much longer I can stay here. A child in my class wore the same filthy outfit to school for two weeks in a row. Vermin were crawling out from under his shirtsleeves. I wanted to take him home with me and give him a bath, but I'm not allowed."

Institutionalized Disrespect

Teachers have never been high in the social pecking order of the United States, but the noble, literature-loving spinster of earlier eras was at least respected. In modern times, "dissing" teachers has become a national pastime for politicians who do not look to them for votes, for academics who are pleasurably horrified by reports of their limitations, and by people who think (not without reason) that the profession protects incompetents. This widespread lack of respect for teachers discourages intelligent, self-respecting people from entering the field and drives many good teachers out of the classroom.

Among the teachers who stay on the job are those who love teaching so much that the most horrendous working conditions cannot diminish their joy. There are also those who hunker down to a minimal level of performance because most school districts have built minimal performance into curricula, tests, textbooks, and teacher evaluation. For them, fighting the system is just not worth the effort. Even the brightest, best-educated, most energetic teachers can be worn down over the years by the spiritually corroding effects of disrespect.

Many thoughtful citizens know that teaching is a very hard job and try to show their appreciation in small, personal ways. Most schools and school districts choose someone to be Teacher of the Year. PTAs have "teacher appreciation" committees and often plan end-of-year ceremonies to thank teachers for their work. States participate in annual Teacher of the Year contests, and the Council of Chief State School Officers has been conducting a national Teacher of the Year program for many years. In the 1980s, many corporate donors began to support teacher-recognition programs, offering the winners cars, scholarships, trips, summer study programs, and various other benefits. These programs are well-intentioned and do encourage the recipients. At the same time, however, they tend to reinforce the lowly status of teachers. There is no Lawyer Appreciation Week or Dentist of the Year program. Corporations do not give free cars to architects who design marvelous buildings, or to doctors who invent life-saving therapies. Moreover, the happy winners of teaching awards return to work situations that by their very nature do not honor their wisdom and skills.

Nearly every institutional arrangement in the present system undermines the notion of the teacher as professional. Frank Murray, dean of the School of Education at the University of Delaware, and Daniel Fallon, dean of the School of Education at Texas A&M University, write: "A clear example of our lack of confidence is that we hire, on the average, one professional to work outside the classroom to supervise and guide the work of each teacher who works in a classroom. Moreover, the regular assignment of routine, low-level non-teaching tasks to teachers, on the view that it is cost-effective to have the teacher do them, only confirms the conclusion that nowhere is teaching seen as a profession."[2]

Emily Sachar, a reporter at *Newsday*, took a year off to teach eighth-grade math at a Brooklyn junior high school and wrote about the pervasive mistrust of teachers:

> I am still stunned by how little teachers are trusted by the school administration. I had to post a time card each morning and each afternoon, and I had to stay in school until the dismissal bell rang, even after I was done teaching for the day. I could not get tests mimeo-

graphed or order my year allotment of supplies without a supervisor's approval.

     Chalk was handed out a box at a time. And
"out of order" signs were taped to the copying ma-
chines even when they worked; teachers were not permitted to use them. Materials for students were
rationed even more stringently. For the first three
weeks of the year, we were not allowed to distribute
textbooks. Yet we were also limited to one class set—
35 copies—of any worksheet. If I needed worksheets
for more than one class, I had to forbid the students
from writing on them and retrieved them for my next
class. A supervisor had to sign off on anything I
wanted to have copied.[3]

Sink or Swim

The profession's treatment of its own novices ranges from off-
handedness to sadism. Student teachers are paired with cooperating
teachers or mentors of uneven quality, because neither principals
(who sometimes get to choose them) nor unions (which often have
negotiated control over selection) have any sense of themselves as
responsible agents for grooming the next generation of teachers.
There are some exceptions, of course, but they are few and far
between.

     The American tradition is to assign the first-year elementary
school teacher to the most incorrigible class. The teacher with seniority gets herself reassigned to a gifted class, or to a school in the
pleasant suburbs. First-year secondary teachers are usually assigned
to the low-track kids or to subjects they did not prepare for, and
often their mentors, if there are any, teach full schedules and have
no time to observe or help the newcomers. Beginning teaching in
America is like being thrown into a piranha tank.

Unrelenting Schedules, Perfect Isolation

Once beginning teachers work their way past the harrowing first
year or two, they settle into a work routine that most teachers think

is normal because it is the only one they know. Elementary teachers are shut up in classrooms with their fidgety students for unbroken hours on end. "I don't have a five-and-a-half-hour attention span, so how could a 10 year old," writes Sarah Mosle. Her job was to teach the second shift (12:15–5:30). One of her students found a bug in his half-eaten snack and threw up. Mosle sent for a mop and pail, but they never arrived. "What was so unnerving was not any particular crisis, but the sense of being all alone," Mosle writes. Even for elementary teachers in more typical schools, finding time merely to go to the bathroom or telephone a parent can be a minor feat.

In the secondary schools, there is usually a "planning period," but few teachers have quiet places to work, with materials close at hand. Even if they do, the planning period seldom coincides with the planning periods of the colleagues they need to work with.

Teaching in America combines the deadliest and most demeaning aspects of assembly-line work with the loneliest and most demanding aspects of professional work. Even in a school with rich and smart kids, supportive parents, a strong and respectful principal, a harmonious faculty, and abundant supplies and equipment, the demoralizing reality is that virtually all teachers are tied down in classrooms for nearly the whole school day. In addition to their class-related paperwork, they are compelled to complete vast numbers of administrative forms and reports, which for the most part are not read, analyzed, or put to productive use.

Harold W. Stevenson of the University of Michigan has spent a decade on comparative studies of American, Chinese, and Japanese educational systems. Comparing the lives of elementary teachers in the three countries, he says, "on the basis of our observations and interviews, we have concluded that being an elementary school teacher in the United States is extraordinarily difficult, and that the demands made by American society exhaust even the most energetic among them. American teachers are expected to spend the whole school day, with only a few breaks, in charge of their class. They are not only expected to teach the children during these hours, but also to be responsive to the children's psychological and academic needs."[4] Beijing teachers were incredulous when Stevenson explained to them how American teachers work: "When, they asked, did the teachers prepare their lessons, consult with other teachers about teaching techniques, grade students' papers, and work with individuals students who were having difficulties?" American teachers usually grade papers and prepare lessons at night, when they are tired. In Japan and China, where teachers are responsible for classes only part of the day, that work is done at school in professional surroundings. "American teachers have neither the time nor the incentive to share experiences with each other or to benefit from hearing about the successes and failures that others have had in teaching particular lessons," Stevenson writes. But in Asia, he reports, teaching is more of a group endeavor: "Teachers consult with each other frequently about teaching techniques. More experienced teachers help newer teachers. Head teachers in each grade organize meetings to discuss teaching techniques and to devise lesson plans and handouts. The group may spend hours designing a single lesson, or discussing how to frame questions that will elicit the greatest understanding in their pupils." Because Asian teachers have so much time during the school day to polish their lessons, Asian students find their lessons more interesting than American students, who often report that school is boring. "Their demanding daily schedule places serious constraints on the ability of American teachers to create exciting, well-organized lessons by themselves," Stevenson concludes. By contrast, he observes: "It is the widespread excellence of Asian class lessons that is so impressive." (It should be noted here that many Asian teachers are not college graduates.)

Working conditions for teachers depend, in part, on working conditions for children. In the United States, students are also treated like cogs in the great school machine. They are expected to sit down and learn for unbroken hours on end, and their attention falters. Asian children, by contrast, get a recess after each class. They play and relax with each other. Social life is incorporated into the school day. These recesses, Stevenson says, may explain why Asian children are better behaved and more attentive in class than American children. Asian children, he reports, are under less stress than American children (contrary to a widespread myth in the United States), more eager to go to school each day, cannot wait for vacation to end, and are more willing to do homework in the evenings because their social needs have been satisfied during the day.

Asian teachers also work with a national curriculum. Since all third-grade teachers or all chemistry teachers are teaching the same material at the same time, teachers can consult with peers anywhere in the national system about how best to teach it. The national government provides in-service training to deepen teachers' knowledge. And because the national curriculum does not change very often, teachers find it worthwhile to hone their teaching skills in relation to particular content and how students are responding to it. In these ways, a national curriculum works to conserve and consolidate teachers' knowledge and skills. By contrast, American teachers are kept in a perennial uproar by constantly changing curricula, textbooks, and testing programs.

Systematic Disregard for Academic Qualifications

In many states, a teacher who is prepared to teach English may be assigned, at the convenience of an administrator, to teach history or math. Almost anywhere, a teacher who majored in biology is presumed able to teach physics, if no trained physics teacher is available. When assigned to teach subjects they know little about, an amazing number of teachers enroll in night classes or spend countless hours boning up on the foundations. Often, however, principals reassign them to still other subjects they know little about. Unions, which should be in the vanguard of protest against the misassignment of teachers, usually go along in order to save members' jobs. Inherent in this practice is an institutional disrespect for knowledge and for students, who will be taught by someone who is one chapter ahead of the class.

The devaluation of a teacher's subject matter knowledge is built into the American educational system in other ways. What teachers know about their subjects before they are hired is not a serious topic of inquiry in the vast majority of school systems. Neither is there any ongoing effort to update practicing teachers' knowledge of the subjects they teach. The in-service training catalogues in most school districts show many opportunities to learn generic techniques, how to teach minority or handicapped young-

sters, or how to use the state's newly adopted basal readers. All of
these things may be useful, but the fact remains that content doesn't
get much play in most in-service training programs. Math and
science workshops for elementary teachers have made an appear-
ance lately, and perhaps that is a portent of things to come.

Teachers who go back to school usually do so in order to
qualify for salary increases, which are pegged to credit hours and
degrees. Since personnel offices are usually indifferent to the kind
of degree earned, harassed teachers often opt for an M.A. in educational administration, which is much less taxing than one in zool-
ogy or linguistics. Many teachers do take advanced degrees in their
specialties, and many enroll (for no salary credit) in summer workshops offered by their subject matter associations, but they do so in
spite of the official incentive system.

Students Off the Hook

The most debilitating condition of work for teachers is of recent
origin. It is the notion that the teacher, not the student, is solely
responsible for how much students learn. Reforms in the early 1980s
carried the businessman's idea of accountability: the workers
(teachers) will work harder if they are given incentives (merit pay)
for producing results (higher student test scores), and if they are
punished (no salary increase) for failing to produce results.

The system was also designed to hold students accountable.
Students who did not pass the tests were to be held back or denied
diplomas. But the economic and political consequences of holding
students back soon became evident. Taxpayers were obliged to pay
for an additional year of education for every student who was held
back. After the first wave of "promotional gates" programs (New
York City was the site of the most notable example), accommoda-
tions were made. Instead of repeating an entire year, students who
failed went to catch-up summer programs. School leaders kept the
same old tests year after year, rather than buying new, "renormed"
tests, because they had discovered that teachers gradually became
familiar with the test items and could arm their students with the
right answers. Teachers were hounded to "teach to the tests." Grad-

ually, scores improved. Flunk rates dropped. For all practical purposes, students were off the hook.

Teachers were also let off the hook, at least in formal ways. The "carrots" and "sticks" associated with these accountability systems soon disappeared. Merit pay had a short life, either because teachers so massively disapproved of the criteria for selecting recipients or because school boards reneged. The "stick" of withholding pay increases was seldom applied and gradually got lost in the soft muddy bottom of American education.

The residue of this version of accountability has been toxic, however. Most teachers believe, rightly or wrongly, that they and they alone are being held accountable for students' success. The 1980s accountability movement, with its emphasis on the teacher's responsibility for student learning, has put the finishing touches on an already grotesque situation. Teachers are at the mercy of their students because it is the students who determine a teacher's success, not the other way around.

If the teacher assigns easy work and the student gets a good grade, the student sees no reason to push himself. Everybody is happy. If the teacher assigns difficult work and the student fails, the parents are apt to stage a nasty scene. Increasingly, parents appeal their children's grades to higher authorities, and teachers' judgments are often overturned. In such a climate, teachers can and do strike subtle bargains with students: easy work and passing grades, in exchange for good behavior.[5] There are now massive, systemic disincentives for American teachers to demand the intellectual performance that the reformers, and elite members of the general public, claim to want.

Even before the accountability revolution of the 1980s, American students' motivation to work in school was weak. Stevenson's comparisons of American and Asian attitudes toward ability, achievement, and effort make the point very clearly. Stevenson found that most American mothers think their children are "above average" and doing well in school, even when they are not; their children share those views. Asian parents, by contrast, do not generally see their children as exceptional and are not highly satisfied with their school performance:

When mothers are as positive as American mothers seem to be about their children's current academic performance and cognitive abilities, and when their children share these beliefs, children may find little incentive to strive for higher levels of achievement. The higher motivation of Asian children to work hard in school may be strongly influenced by their perception that their cognitive and academic abilities are not especially remarkable. In order to be successful in school, they believe they will have to work hard.[6]

According to Stevenson, the willingness of Asian children to work hard in school is also influenced by the Confucian belief that effort can modify human development: "Every Chinese and Japanese school child can quote mottos emphasizing the importance of diligence and hard work. 'The roughest stone can be made smooth through years of daily polishing.' 'The slow bird must start out early.' "[7]

American parents and children seem to believe that innate ability determines how much students learn, at least in mathematics. Students with "low ability" cannot learn as much as students with "high ability." Stevenson does not attribute these views to American reverence for psychometrics and belief in the immutability of IQ scores, but these are at least plausible hypotheses to explain what appears to be a fairly recent collapse of the nineteenth-century American belief in personal responsibility and hard work.

American students' motivation to work in school has been further eroded by lowered college admission standards. Standards for admission to the top colleges are still high, and top high school students are motivated to seek spots in these colleges, but too many colleges are scrambling for the tuition of too few students, and it is now possible for a student to get into some kind of college regardless of grades or SAT and ACT scores.

American employers rarely examine the transcripts of the students they hire; even if they wanted to, it might take them months to pry a transcript out of the school bureaucracy. For most employers, proof that the student earned a high school diploma, combined with their own judgment of character, is usually sufficient. Except for students whose parents continually reinforce the connection between school work and the good life, American students have few incentives to work hard and earn good grades.

Can Working Conditions Be Improved?

Some of the debilitating working conditions for teachers are deeply rooted in the American character and political structure. We have an anti-intellectual tradition, and it may take many decades for us to become a nation like Japan that values learning for its own sake. Our evolution into a society that unambiguously regards schooling as important may be speeded by global economic competition and the increasing knowledge requirements for a dynamic work environment. Working-class parents, in particular, may begin to see the value of schooling when their adult children are living at home, unable to find a job that pays a family wage. As the economic benefits of knowledge increase, the public may be pushed toward a greater respect for teachers' knowledge.

Although we have a long and deep tradition of local control over the schools, the movement toward national standards has at least begun. If national standards take hold, parents will have an objective point of reference for judging their children's achievement and their schools' effectiveness. Some may begin to question whether their children and schools are doing as well as they now imagine.

The trade-unionist stance of the National Education Association and the American Federation of Teachers is also a long and deep tradition. It is hard to imagine either organization replacing trade-union ideology with professional standards, in the short run. Although "working conditions" are within the scope of collective bargaining, union versions of working conditions often include some of the anti-intellectual, antiprofessional stances already discussed in this chapter: strict application of seniority; blind rotation as the basis for extra-pay, extra-duty assignments; the habit of ignoring teachers' misassignments when jobs are at stake. In hard economic times, unions are not likely to redefine working conditions, especially when they must flex every muscle merely to keep their members from losing economic ground or from being laid off.

It is possible to imagine that a younger group of union leaders, less wedded to trade-union ideology, might begin to support a more professional definition of working conditions. The Toledo Federation of Teachers and the Cincinnati Federation of Teachers (CFT) have negotiated peer-review programs that either help or get rid of incompetent teachers. The contract between the Cincinnati schools and the CFT provides for the selection of "lead teachers" and "mentors" according to professional criteria. The union, the Cincinnati schools, and the University of Cincinnati have joined in the development of professional practice schools, where teaching interns will spend an entire year learning how to teach. The contract also forbids out-of-field assignment. Such subject-based organizations as the National Council of Teachers of Mathematics and the National Science Teachers' Association are now defining higher standards for the education and licensure of math and science teachers and may begin to exert a counterpressure against state manipulation of licensing standards and the administrative practice of misassigning teachers.

Other debilitating working conditions are not deeply rooted and so seem more amenable to change. The Lake Wobegon effect, named for Garrison Keillor's fictional Minnesota town where "all the children are above average," is a recent development. One need not go very far back to a find a time when Americans understood that everybody is *not* above average, and when they believed that effort paid off. Another relatively new belief is that genetic throws of the dice outweigh effort and persistence. With enlightened leadership, it should be possible to restore the view that students are also responsible for their learning and to restore the delicate balance of power between teachers and students.

Testing as an Adverse Working Condition, Assessment as a Spur

The stranglehold of state-mandated multiple-choice tests on teachers and teaching is well documented. The rising tide of standardized multiple-choice tests is beginning to subside, however. Many states are developing or borrowing new tests, which measure more than superficial recall of isolated bits of information. The National

Assessment of Educational Progress is moving in the same direction. Students are being asked to exhibit their knowledge through projects and presentations, to show that they can apply knowledge to novel and complex tasks, and to demonstrate their growth over time through work portfolios. Writing is being assessed by asking students to write. As these new tests become part of the educational scene, teachers will be freer to teach the things that really matter, and to teach for understanding. They will be less driven to cram their students full of soon-to-be-forgotten trivia.

Creating assessments that drive teaching in the right direction will not be quick or easy. Development, administration, and scoring of these improved assessment tools will be very expensive, and it is not yet clear that policy makers and the public are willing to pay the price. The new models of assessment also presume major changes in curricula, teaching methods, and textbooks. Therefore, progress is likely to be slow. Parents and the press will need to be persuaded that the results of these more complex assessments will be better than the meaningless numbers that everyone has come to rely on.

The main ingredient in improved working conditions is time—time for teachers to think about what they are doing and to work with other teachers, individual students, and parents. Time means money, which in turn means taxpayers' resistance.

The case for lengthening the school day and the school year, in order to provide that time, is probably easier to make now than ever before. The vast majority of American parents have full-time jobs; many scramble for makeshift after-school child care, and others worry about the safety of their unsupervised kids in the late afternoons and summers. According to Theodore Sizer, what parents most want is for their kids to be with decent companions in safe places. If supervised socialization were built into the school day, then some of parents' deepest concerns would be allayed. Taxpayers might be more willing to pay the price if there were offsetting reductions in the number of kibitzers who oversee the work of teachers—an overseeing that, so far, has not produced very impressive results.

A longer school day and a longer school year are likely to be opposed by those teachers who became teachers so that they could be with their own children in the afternoons and summers. Cynics say that teachers want only more pay and shorter hours, and any casual observer can see that the teachers' parking lot is often empty within minutes after the students' day ends. But the sullenness implicit in speedy exits and work-to-the-rule actions is a predictable response to isolation and disrespect. If teaching hours were interspersed with hours of collegial work, many teachers who now walk out on the dot might prefer to be at school.

Many other teachers would prefer year-round school. Some believe that the profession will not be respected until teachers work full-time. Some think that children lose too much ground over the summers. Some would like to be in a professionally enriching, intellectually stimulating environment that can be achieved only with a longer work day.

Teachers' isolation is beginning to be addressed in the many initiatives to "restructure" schools and "empower" teachers. In the best of these, time is allocated for teachers to plan together and make decisions about issues related to teaching work. But deciding and planning are rather muscular concepts, borrowed from government or business, and seem to miss the mark for teaching work. These activities do not capture the essence of what the Asian teachers do when they have time together—reflect, reenact, refine.

In the worst cases, school districts have adopted school-site governance and saddled local faculties with managerial responsibilities. Predictably, many of these faculties have decided they do not like school-site governance after all. Perhaps that was the manipulative intent of school district leaders. After these faculties exhausted themselves drafting budgets and executing contracts for the repair of buildings, they bailed out of the projects.

Nevertheless, a number of teachers in many places, for the first time, have been allowed out of their classrooms and encouraged to work together in teams, or as faculties. A small number of them are taking the opportunity to explore the fine-grained details of teaching and learning and to create interdisciplinary curricula. But, according to Phillip Schlecty, a national leader in the restructuring movement, whole school districts will have to become involved in changing rules, roles, and relationships if the movement is to succeed. Meanwhile, a very few individual schools have created working conditions for teachers that truly foster growth. This movement, more than any other, carries the promise of better teaching in our nation's schools.

Current efforts to recruit bright and able people into teaching, to deepen their knowledge of academic subjects, and to extend their years of training will be to no avail if teachers' working conditions do not improve. These better-educated people will simply leave teaching if they are not treated as professionals, if the knowledge they have acquired is not respected, and if their authority is systematically undermined.

10

An Unregulated Monopoly

One of the major obstacles to the improvement of teacher education is the failure of the states to shut down inferior teacher education programs and the states' unwillingness to abide by their own standards for licensing teachers. As employers of teachers, states have a conflict of interest. They want qualified teachers, but they also want a plentiful supply of cheap labor. When the chips are down, they opt for plentiful and cheap, rather than qualified. Unions also have a conflict of interest. They are more interested in preserving the jobs and perks of dues-paying members than in professional standards for current and future teachers. More often than not, unions work to keep a failed system in place.

State Accreditation of Teacher Education

If you loathe teacher education as you observe it in your nearby university, and if you know teachers you think should not have been let out of high school, let alone college, you should know that your state has authorized that school of education to operate and has licensed those teachers. As a taxpaying citizen, you support a state board of education and a bureaucracy that purport to ensure the quality of teacher training and the integrity of licensing requirements but do not do so. You may have been led to believe that your state has recently raised standards; but, as this chapter shows, there are too many built-in disincentives to quality and too many regulatory escape hatches to make these initiatives as promising as they appear.

One important thing to notice is that teaching is the only profession still regulated by state political officials. The states long ago delegated their power to define the educational standards for every other profession or trade, from medicine to cosmetology to practitioner groups. When practitioner groups demand changes to upgrade the education and training of their future colleagues, the training institutions fork over the money without a quibble.

In the teaching field, however, there is no national professional group with that kind of power. The only equivalent organization in teaching is the National Council for Accreditation of Teacher Education. For most of its existence, NCATE's accreditation process has been as toothless as the one run by state political authorities.

In 1988, however, NCATE adopted new standards, which far exceed those of most states. Since 1988, NCATE has actually denied accreditation to about 30 percent of the schools of education that have sought its stamp of approval. Since state bureaucracies still have the final word, however, a university that does not want to spend time and money meeting NCATE's standards can ignore them. Review by NCATE is voluntary, and only 500 of the nation's 1,200 teacher education institutions have chosen to be reviewed. Under the shelter of state standards, an inferior school of education can continue to operate, and its graduates can continue to become licensed teachers if they pass the state's (undemanding) tests. Few states have chosen to scrap their own ineffective systems and abide by NCATE's standards, but the final outcome of NCATE's struggle to gain moral (if not constitutional) authority over teacher education still hangs in the balance. Ultimately, the success of this battle depends on the states' willingness to delegate control.

"Authorization to operate" or "approval" is granted when a

state gives a school of education permission to operate, on the basis of standards that the state has devised. State education agencies continually tinker with the standards. Historically, such tinkering has often come in response to demands from state boards of education, state legislators, or teacher educators themselves. For example, a state legislator might introduce a bill requiring all future teachers to take a course in state history—a requirement that has been politically impossible to resist. More recently, state requirements have been imposed in response to the ideas of "education governors" or special interest groups. Such groups can usually persuade legislators to require courses on hot social issues—drug abuse, AIDS prevention, or whatever—all fine ideas, but all at the expense of future teachers' general education.

Over the decades, there has been a steady accumulation of required courses, and of things to be taught in those courses. If many education programs are overblown and incoherent, it is largely because the states have made them so. Worse, since requirements differ from state to state, a teacher licensed in one state may not be able to get licensed in another. The crazy quilt of state-determined teacher education and licensing standards impedes the flow of teachers from areas of surplus to areas of shortage.

In recent years, the poor quality of teacher education has become a rallying cry in the education reform movement. A few states have tried to undo some of the harm done by their past regulatory excesses. In an effort to get a smarter group of people into teaching, or at least to prevent virtually illiterate people from enrolling in teacher education, many states now require students to pass basic skills tests before being admitted to schools of education. Although that is a fairly minimal standard, the imposition of such tests does seem to have cut down on the number of minimally educated people in education programs. Many states have pared down the number of required education courses, increased the number of subject matter courses, or required more of both. The emphasis, however, is still on quantity, and there is still no assurance of quality. A few states have expressed the intention to switch from an "input" model to an "output" model. But so far, nobody has been able to define what "output" consists of, or to come up with the funds to measure it. Thus far, reform efforts have been unremarkable.

Optimists think that the time is ripe for a national consensus on teacher education and for agreement on a national system. A national, professionally driven accreditation system could make teacher education more rigorous by insulating it from the local political pressures that keep inferior programs in business. Attracting out-of-state teachers would be easier. The forty-nine states that maintain accreditation bureaucracies would save money by letting NCATE do the job. The idea of a national system has been endorsed by the Council of Chief State School Officers, the Vocational Education Association, and other organizations. Pessimists, however, think that the states are unlikely to surrender control to an "outside" group, even though the states have surrendered control to outside groups in the case of every other licensed profession.

At present, most governors seem unlikely to support a national system of quality control. Since education has become a hot political issue, governors have competed with one another to make splashy moves in the regulation of teacher education, and they are not likely to give up such a political opportunity. Moreover, governors do not seem to trust teacher educators. Lynn Olson of *Education Week*, the author of a series of articles on teacher education, quotes an unnamed observer: "I think governors are frustrated by teacher education. They don't know how to get hold of it. They don't know what it is. They're convinced that the people who come out of it are not very good. And so they're not about to give up on the controls they perceive they have."[1]

An Unregulated Monopoly

However well-intentioned the actions of governors, legislators, and state boards of education, the fact remains that teacher education is virtually unregulated. This is so because no education school, however dreadful, is ever closed down. Perhaps it is slapped on the wrist for this or that failing, but it is not put out of business. Politicians rescue schools that are threatened with the state's disapproval. They also think that it is their prerogative to intervene when some constituent's sweet daughter has flunked out of an education school in their district.

State education agencies nevertheless make a big show of

regulating the quality of schools of education. Numerous bureau-crats are required to keep the show on the road. In every state, they require schools of education to engage in periodic self-study and to produce massive documentation on faculty credentials, course syllabi, student characteristics, physical facilities, number of library books, student/faculty ratios, and other "objective" indicators of quality. The regulators assemble, train, and deploy visiting teams, usually composed of teacher educators, school administrators, and teachers. The teams go out and visit schools of education and then produce massive reports that have no significant consequences. The system is designed to approve schools of education, and approve it does.

David C. Smith, dean of the college of education at the University of Florida at Gainesville, studied the results of state accreditation programs in the southern states, which have the most stringent requirements for teacher education. He found that "no institution had been denied authority to prepare teachers in the past 10 years." [2]

In his exhaustive study of teacher education, John Goodlad makes it clear that state regulators have not achieved what a citizen might reasonably expect of them: consistency of quality in all state-controlled teacher education programs. Some schools of education find creative ways of getting around foolish or inconsistent regulations. Others slavishly follow state prescriptions. Goodlad reports the case of a school of education that achieved a reputation for being a "quick and dirty" place to get certification because its methods courses "repetitiously taught [students] how to plan and teach a unit according to state specifications." Goodlad sets forth a principle articulated by his colleague Roger Soder: "When rewards and outcomes remain constant, competition drives quality down. The principle is strengthened when those outcomes are simplistic." [3]

State approval of teacher education takes no account of the arts and sciences portion of a teacher's education and has no way to influence its quality. This is the very portion that the educated public complains about most vociferously. The inspection of this portion of a teacher's education is left to the regional associations that accredit colleges and universities. If one were to judge that inspection system on the basis of what holders of bachelor's degrees know, it would not look much better than the state system for inspecting teacher education.

Nobody should be comforted by recent state or university mandates requiring those who enter or exit education programs to maintain higher grade-point averages. In a swashbuckling denunciation of teacher education in Texas in 1979, Gene Lyons made an observation that is as true today as it was then: "Grade inflation is built into the system." Lyons explains: "What is the cause of grade inflation? It is simple: all public colleges, and all their divisions and departments, get their operating budgets from the state according to formulas based almost entirely on the number of students enrolled. . . . The departments get more money by getting bigger, less money by getting smaller."[4]

As can be seen in the sketches of education schools in this book, even when teacher educators are willing to play the role of gatekeeper, their efforts are often resisted or totally blocked by higher authorities in the university, or by a faculty senate. A dean of a school of education recently told me that he would like to wash out half the students in his program, but even if the tenure system allowed him to put half his education colleagues out of work, the higher-ups in his university would reverse his decision. The reason: schools of education are "cash cows" for many universities and colleges. Arts and sciences faculties depend on the funds brought in by education students to increase or maintain the number of faculty members. In addition, arts and science faculties use teacher education programs as dumping grounds for students they do not want.

Licensure

Licenses to teach are granted according to licensing rules that states set for themselves. Although program approval and licensure are separate processes, the states have made licensure contingent on graduation from state-approved education programs. New Jersey became an exception in 1983, when it created an "alternate route" into teaching for people with subject matter degrees. Forty states now have some form of "alternate route" certification.

Over the past decade, political leaders in most of the states have loudly trumpeted higher standards for licensure. At least thirty-three states now require graduates of education programs to pass licensing tests. But many of the tests are merely rock-bottom literacy tests, which screen out only those who lack rudimentary skills in arithmetic, reading, and writing.

Please notice that many of those who fail these minimal tests have probably been awarded college degrees by one of the public universities that your taxes support. Schools of education are usually blamed for the failure of their graduates on these low-level tests, but it is well to remember that professors of English and mathematics gave these students passing grades, without which they would not have been allowed to enter education programs.

Twenty-two states require applicants for licensure to pass a test with an impressive name—the National Teachers Examination (NTE). Results on NTE tests of subject matter knowledge do say something about a future high school teacher's grasp of a discipline, but the portions on general and professional knowledge are barely more than tricky reading tests. The people who do not pass these portions are usually those who have not been taught how to decode the strange language of psychometricians. A new and improved NTE is on the way, but it is too soon to know whether it will provide a warrant for competence.

Even if the much-ballyhooed licensure tests did represent a route to what the public understands by "higher standards," and even if the internship requirements recently added to state licensing systems were what they appear to be, the states still maintain enough legal loopholes in their licensing rules to permit almost anyone who is not a felon to get a teaching job when shortages of teachers exist. The folk notion that "anybody can teach" is truly enshrined in the licensing system in the United States.

In all but eight states, politicians and bureaucrats determine the standards for licensing teachers. In forty-two states, therefore, state officials decide the number of licensure categories, what tests will be administered, and what the "cut score" will be. They determine when licenses will be granted—after graduation from a teacher education program, after the passing of a test, after a supervised internship program, or after one or more years of satisfactory teaching. They make rules requiring teachers to be assigned to the courses they are qualified to teach, and then they set forth endless exceptions to the rules. They decide whether an applicant who is licensed in another state can teach in another state, and under what conditions.

The most important thing to notice about teacher licensing in the United States is that teaching is among the very few professions or skilled trades where unlicensed people are allowed to practice. A hospital lacking a qualified doctor would be required to close down lest patients be subjected to treatment by an unlicensed person. An unlicensed electrician is not allowed to work on your household electrical system. Engineers-without-benefit-of-clergy can do engineering work, but only under the supervision of those who have met professional standards.

In the case of education, though, the conventional wisdom is that schools cannot be closed down for lack of licensed teachers, because the state has a constitutional responsibility to maintain an educational system. When faced with shortages, states quietly lower the cut scores on their tests, so as to create more licensed teachers. The public is usually none the wiser. States issue "emergency," "temporary," "provisional," and "long-term substitute" licenses to fill vacancies, or they look the other way when local superintendents wantonly violate the already lax rules about out-of-field assignment of teachers. In most states, the local superintendent merely has to say (not prove) that a qualified person cannot be found.

Loopholes in state regulations leave the way open for local school districts to perform a number of antieducational acts. They can, with impunity, hire friends and relatives of school board members to teach on emergency certificates. They can ignore the fact that someone on a temporary certificate has failed to amass the proper credits within the required period. They can protect the retirement benefits of a teacher who is near retirement, but no longer needed in her specialty, by assigning her to a course that she is utterly unprepared to teach, and they can justify that action as humane.

Loopholes also permit school systems to cope with one of the most brutal realities of American education. Few graduates of education programs are willing to work in big city school systems or in remote rural schools. According to Martin Haberman, a professor of education at the University of Wisconsin at Milwaukee, "70 percent of the newly certified college graduates [in Wisconsin] do not take jobs. In Minnesota, it is 68 percent." Haberman goes on to say:

> In states across America, the majority of regularly cer-
> tified graduates seek positions where they are not
> needed (small towns and suburbs) and avoid teaching
> in the districts where they are needed (metropolitan
> districts and remote rural areas). Traditional teacher
> education programs in urban universities are no dif-
> ferent or better, and even add to their irrelevance by
> ignoring the continuing needs of their cooperating
> school districts for teachers with particular specializa-
> tions. ("After all, we can't tell our students what to
> major in.") Universities cannot provide the teachers
> America needs because, in traditional programs, the
> clients are the tuition paying students and not the
> children and youth of America.[5]

Haberman believes that schools of education have a vested interest in allowing tuition-paying students to graduate whether or not they are fit to teach in the cities, and he is right. For thirty years, Haberman has been involved in the development of "alternate route" licensure, especially for those preparing to teach in urban schools with high concentrations of poor and minority children. "Children and youths need teachers who want to be with them and who believe they can learn," he says, and such teachers are being recruited through "alternate route" programs. Most such teachers are older than the typical college graduate and far more likely to be mature enough for the job. Moreover, Haberman says, principals, parents, and pupils "rate them more highly because they speak the same cultural language as their students." In a Texas "alternate route" program that Haberman helped to develop, 58 percent of the can-didates are members of minority groups, as compared to 5 percent in traditional programs. "After six years [of the Texas "alternate route" program], we now see alternative teachers as school leaders and change agents."[6]

The "Alternate Route"

In response to widespread criticism of teachers working on emergency and temporary licenses, at least thirty-three states have designed a more dignified exception to their licensure rules—"alternate route" programs for college graduates who did not complete required sequences of education courses. In the best of situations, "alternate route" teachers take summer courses, attend weekly seminars, and are coached by highly accomplished mentors who are trained, paid, and given time to observe and coach the trainees.

At present, there are few of these best situations. Some "alternate route" programs are barely distinguishable from emergency certification. Most of the teachers chosen to mentor "alternate route" teachers carry full or nearly full teaching loads. They "mentor" in the hallways between classes. Their selection, as in California, is often determined by union seniority and rotation principles, rather than by professional standards. A great mentor will be tossed out after one year so that somebody else can have a turn at the extra pay that comes with the assignment. Some states that initially funded "alternate route" programs later withdrew the funds. Where a state requires school districts to pay for the training of "alternate route" teachers, superintendents can evade this responsibility by pleading insufficient funds. There is still no mechanism for holding the educational system accountable when it comes to the proper induction of either "alternate route" or traditional teachers.

Opponents of "alternate route" programs would agree with Haberman that the traditional system of teacher education is broken. Haberman says that he is not interested in reforming the system. Others, like Arthur Wise, president of NCATE, are intensely interested in reform. Wise thinks that the system can and must be fixed. He challenges the logic of state officials who simultaneously tighten standards (by raising entrance and exit standards for students in schools of education and by imposing licensure tests) and loosen them (by designing "quick entry" programs for people who do not choose the ordinary route).

"As long as standards can be relaxed, the supply of teachers is unlimited," Wise says. "An unlimited supply of teachers will depress both wages and prestige. Under these conditions, most teachers will be drawn from groups that have few or no other options."[7] Moreover, Wise points out, very few teachers are being recruited through "alternate route" programs. For better or for worse, the overwhelming number of people who aspire to teaching jobs enroll in and are shaped by teacher education programs. Given that the schools of education are where most of the future teachers are, Wise and others see no choice but to fix the system.

A National System of Quality Control

Arthur Wise's solution to the problem is complex and farseeing. He advocates a rigorous national system of teacher accreditation (NCATE) run by the profession itself rather than by the states. He believes that teaching will become what we want it to become only when preparation for it follows the pattern of other learned professions—a basic liberal arts education; rigorous training in a professional school; a lengthy supervised internship in a school designed for that purpose; knowledge tests that command public respect (as state bar examinations do); and performance assessment prior to licensing (as in a medical internship). Rigorous training must be based on research whenever there is compelling evidence that some things work better than others, or, in the absence of research, on professional consensus. An acceptable program, Wise says, would make people feel comfortable about going to teach in cities. Designated "professional development schools" in urban centers would be structured to properly induct teachers into the human and cultural realities of teaching in those settings.

Wise argues that "alternate route" programs, no less than emergency or temporary licenses, undermine professionalization by postponing the day when the teaching profession has the clout to put terrible schools of education out of business and the power to prevent unqualified people from being given the title of teacher.

Wise proposes to address the shortage of teachers by creating three categories of people who work with students in classrooms: instructors, professional teachers, and national board–certified teachers. Instructors could be any college graduates that school systems choose to hire, according to their own criteria. They could become professional teachers, but not without meeting the standards required for that rank. Professional teachers would be those who have graduated from NCATE-approved education programs and who have satisfied state licensure standards. State professional-standards boards with teacher majorities would design and police licensure standards, replacing the licensing boards run by officials who have a vested interest in keeping costs down and the supply of teachers up. National board–certified teachers would supervise the work of instructors (hired to relieve shortages) and beginning professional teachers. National board–certified teachers would be those who had submitted themselves to a rigorous assessment developed by the National Board for Professional Teaching Standards (NBPTS). NBPTS is currently defining what highly accomplished teachers should know and be able to do and is developing assessment tools designed to capture the complexity of great teaching. Sometime in 1993 or 1994, NBPTS will begin to certify highly accomplished teachers.

Teacher-Controlled Licensure

The National Education Association (NEA), the dominant teacher organization in most states, has relentlessly lobbied state legislatures to surrender control over teacher licensure to professional-standards boards with teacher majorities. So far, ten state legislatures have established such boards: California, Georgia, Indiana, Iowa, Kentucky, Minnesota, Nevada, North Dakota, Oregon, and Wyoming. The American Federation of Teachers (AFT) generally has opposed the NEA. Only in New York, where the AFT is the dominant teacher organization, did the AFT actively support a failed attempt to establish a professional-standards board with a teacher majority.

The theory behind teacher-controlled professional-standards boards is that teachers have a vested interest in improving the quality of incoming teachers. School administrators, by contrast, are seen to have a vested interest in minimally qualified beginning teachers: they are more plentiful and therefore cheaper to hire. Teacher unions are beginning to support measures to upgrade the academic and professional qualifications of new teachers. Such measures not only will improve the image of the profession but, in time, will also justify raising the salary standards for all teachers. Moreover, the idea of licensing boards effectively controlled by practitioners, although with representation from educational administrators and laymen, conforms to the pattern of quality control in other learned professions.

Theory aside, legislators have been wary of surrendering control. Aside from the fact that nobody surrenders power easily, even when it is badly exercised, there is nervousness about the trade-unionist values that have characterized both the NEA and the AFT for so long. Changes in the teacher unions' philosophy have been slow in coming, but they are beginning to appear at long last. In the mid-1980s, the NEA reversed its historic opposition to prelicensure testing and now supports it. So does the AFT. Both organizations have participated in the development of the revised National Teachers Examination, said to be both more rigorous and more appropriate than the old one. Both organizations support NCATE's efforts to build a rigorous national system of quality control for schools of education, and both appear more ready to support the consequences of such a system—the demise of mediocre schools of education, and denial of jobs to graduates of schools not approved by NCATE.

However much progress has been made in the transition between traditional trade-unionist values and professional standards, the evolution of the two major teacher unions is still incomplete, and there is considerable variation from local chapter to local chapter and from state to state. In general, local affiliates tend to be more militantly trade-unionist because they are closer to the ground and feel compelled to support their dues-paying members, even if the consequences of that support may be seen by outsiders as unprofessional. Nevertheless, a handful of local AFT affiliates, as noted earlier, are moving toward truly professional positions.

That said, neither of the two national unions has yet shown much interest in those aspects of trade-union philosophy that adversely affect student teaching, internships, and the induction of new teachers. Selection of cooperating teachers and mentors still tends to be based on the unionist principle that everybody should get a crack at extra-pay, extra-duty assignments on an equal basis. There is no great push for protected practice on behalf of beginning teachers, probably because such a move would increase the class sizes of dues-paying members. Nor is there much evidence of willingness to work at cleaning up the out-of-field assignment mess, probably because such assignments often save members' jobs. Even though a majority of American teachers now support career ladders (whereby teachers who are judged by their peers to know more are paid more and given time to work with teachers who know less), the NEA generally resists the idea. AFT affiliates are proving to be more friendly to the idea, although the pattern across AFT units is inconsistent.

Many policy makers harbor a grudge against the NEA for its militant opposition to the testing of tenured teachers. (The AFT has earned much public acclaim for supporting such tests.) But, in many cases, the NEA's opposition to "merit pay," based on cheaply gotten-up evaluation schemes that states and localities used to determine "merit," was justified.

In the best of cases, NEA-dominated professional-standards boards have made some marginal improvements, but union opposition to measures that most people would think of as truly professional makes the idea of teacher-controlled standards boards seem premature. In a few AFT local affiliates, there have been revolutionary transformations toward professionalism. But the public's memory of union "thuggishness" is fresh, and its resentment over union protection of poor teachers is sharp. As in the case of physicians, it may take decades for the organized teaching profession to earn the public's trust.

Standards Versus Shortages

On Martin Haberman's side of the argument, "alternate route" programs are getting people into the system quickly and avoiding some of the foolishness that still exists in many (if not most) education programs. Since "alternate route" programs are attracting people who have the desire to teach in urban centers, whereas traditional programs are not, that fact alone argues for opening up the profession to nontraditional recruits. Moreover, "alternate route" programs are attracting far higher percentages of people of color than traditional programs are. People from minority groups are desperately needed for the cultural ballast they bring to the teaching force, and for the sympathetic bonds they more easily form with minority students. Finally, "alternate route" programs make it possible for people who cannot afford to enroll in a year-long postbaccalaureate program to earn a living while they are learning to teach, and vice versa.

Nevertheless, supporters of such programs assume that anything really important in teaching can be learned on the job. Clearly, this is not so. On the average, today's teaching force is highly experienced. If experience alone led to good teaching, we would now have the finest teachers in the world, but we do not. Many veteran teachers make the same mistakes they made in their early years of teaching, because they were improperly trained in the first place, or because their principals lack the knowledge to help them improve their teaching, or because teachers in the United States have few opportunities to learn from more skillful peers.

Haberman and other "alternate route" advocates also assume that a teacher's knowledge of subject matter is self-evident if he or she is a college graduate or passes a test. As we have seen, however, that assumption is unwarranted. Neither the content nor the prevailing teaching methods (lectures, assignments, multiple-choice tests) in liberal arts classes serve teachers well. Gene Lyons, cited earlier, speaks of the degeneration of undergraduate studies:

> In those rare instances where written work is given, grammar, punctuation and style are seen as the business of the English department alone. Nobody in most departments really has any idea whether his students are fully literate; very likely he has never asked them to write. (Perhaps that is just as well, given the kind of jargon-laden, semiliterate humbug that is the going thing in far too many disciplines.) American higher education has been drifting in this direction for some time. The public schools, dominated by Educationists, have already been there for quite a while.[8]

"Alternate route" programs also assume that there is little formal professional training worth having. But there is much evidence that graduates of good traditional education programs are better prepared to manage students' behavior and better able to spot and help students with learning disabilities—a crucial skill in a society that now mainstreams most of its handicapped students. There is also evidence that math and science teachers armed with pedagogical content knowledge, which hardly exists in most school districts at the moment, produce higher-achieving students.

If the objectives of the educational system include the teaching of academic subjects to students who have heretofore not been thought capable of learning them, and if, as it appears, new and better teaching methods are needed to reach hard-to-teach students, then a system that relies exclusively on the existing teaching force to train newcomers will not advance these objectives.

Because there are so few "alternate route" recruits at any given time or place, the formal portions of their training programs are likely to be either blunt indoctrinations into particular teaching methods and curricula or generic "methods" instruction, which is no better than the worst of the traditional methods courses. Alternative conceptions of teaching are not likely to be presented, and content knowledge, if it is considered at all, is divorced from teaching knowledge.[9]

"Alternate route" teachers will learn how to manage a class of unruly kids, how to write lesson plans, and how to work around the insanities of the current system, but their mentors are more likely than not to perpetuate current teaching practices. Thomas Toch summarizes the problem, saying that reformers have "largely sidestepped the difficult but essential task of supplying the capable teachers and fresh instructional strategies needed to reach a wide range of students with the type of challenging academic course work traditionally reserved for the academic and social elites."[10]

Another disadvantage of "alternate route" programs, as well as of temporary or emergency licensing, is that people work their way into tenured positions without meeting any standards of quality control. It is often the school principal who decides whether an "alternate route" teacher will be licensed, and many of today's principals do not look deeply into a teacher's ways of working as long as he or she can keep order and do the paperwork on time. This unaccountable route to licensure, coupled with the overwhelming resistance of teacher unions to the dismissal of tenured teachers, is part of what has brought the system to its present pass.

Wise's proposal to create a category of instructors who must be supervised by highly accomplished, nationally certified teachers has many advantages. School districts could respond to fluctuations in enrollment by hiring college graduates, but those graduates could not become licensed professional teachers without meeting the standards. They would, however, earn enough money to put themselves through the training they would need in order to meet the standards. The training and supervision of instructors would not depend on the energy of individuals like Haberman and the superintendents he works with, or on the vagaries of state and local budgets. Professional norms, rather than trade-unionist norms, would govern placement and training. The public would have some objective evidence that beginners were trained by teachers who knew their subjects deeply, knew how to teach their subject matter to all kinds of students, knew how to weigh the assets and liabilities of various models and methods, deeply understood children and how they think and learn, and knew how to work respectfully with parents and communities.

The three-tiered system that Wise proposes would almost certainly bring more stability to inner-city schools. New recruits leave teaching because they do not know how to relate to the children and know that they are not succeeding. With the right kind of support—built into the system, rather than left to chance—newcomers would be far more likely to stay on the job.

The Long Run, the Short Run, or Both?

The system that Wise envisions is far in the future. Some of its pieces are now being put into place, but the obstacles to its realization are formidable. NCATE operates in a sector of American life that is not noted for its tough-mindedness, and in denying approval to one of every five schools of education it has visited, NCATE has demonstrated more than the usual amount of toughness. As a result, it has lost the participation of some institutions and states. Nevertheless, it has gained the participation of more institutions than ever before. In the years ahead, as the public's appetite for standards increases, NCATE faces the formidable challenge of maintaining a balance between rigorous application of its standards and support of its member organizations.

There are also some questions about the depth of NCATE's review process, and about whether its visiting teams are properly trained and apply NCATE standards consistently. Some of these problems can be cured with time and experience. Others may not be addressed unless NCATE remains in a position to be tough-minded. At the moment, NCATE enjoys some external support from charitable foundations, which seems to indicate that foundation directors see the reform of teacher education as a high priority and see NCATE as a vehicle of reform. But foundations' priorities shift, and NCATE could find its independent stance more difficult to maintain.

In the meantime, "alternate route" programs have responded to crucial and present needs. Lee Shulman of Stanford University has said that the standard routes to teaching are broken, and when the main highway is broken, detours are necessary, but that does not mean that we give up trying to fix the main highway. Policy makers and teacher educators need to recognize the urgency of the plight of children in the nation's inner-city and rural schools, and to throw their support behind "alternate route" programs, making them as sound and rich as possible.

No matter what routes into teaching are sanctioned in the short run, however, there will be no long-term solution to the problem of professional standards in teaching until there has been a major upheaval in one or more well-entrenched systems:

- *State political control over teacher education and licensure.* As long as political control over the accreditation of teacher education and licensure remains unchecked by professional norms, we will continue to have too many schools of education and too many mediocre ones.
- *The tenure system in colleges and universities.* As long as universities cannot fire professors who teach poorly, whose mentality is to weed people out rather than teach them, or who flatly refuse to change the content and methods of their teaching in

ways that benefit teachers, the quality of teacher education and teaching will be seriously undermined.

- *State funding formulas for colleges and universities.* As long as student enrollment is the basis of state funding, most universities will admit unprepared students (and then demand funds for remedial programs). Most university departments will puff up their requirements and then inflate students' grades in order to keep the students. Arts and sciences departments will continue to resist higher standards for students in schools of education.
- *The trade-union mentality of teacher unions.* As long as unions thwart efforts to dismiss poor teachers and reward superior ones, the quality of the teaching force will remain disconcertingly uneven, and the public will remain unwilling to grant more autonomy to teachers. The lack of autonomy will in turn continue to discourage smart people from becoming teachers. As long as unions oppose attempts to distinguish between good and excellent teachers, the choice of mentors to supervise student teachers and beginning teachers will remain haphazard and unprofessional.
- *Employer and/or union domination of teacher licensing.* As long as states and local school districts can exempt themselves from their own licensing standards, and as long as teacher unions oppose rigorous licensing tests and collude with school administrators in the practice of out-of-field assignments, the public will continue to believe that there is no reliable connection between licensure and qualifications.
- *School systems' and unions' norms concerning the treatment of beginning teachers.* As long as school administrators and teacher unions use seniority rather than skill as the basis for choosing cooperating and mentor teachers, the induction of new teachers will continue to be an unreliable process. As long as school systems and unions continue to support "bumping" rights for teachers with greater seniority, the delicate bonds that teachers establish with their students in the beginning of the year will be broken, for the convenience of adults at the expense of students. New teachers will continue to be "bumped" into classes containing the students most in need of expert teaching,

and new teachers will continue to flee the classroom after the first, disastrous year.

Minor upheavals in some of these systems are already underway. A few states have chosen to honor NCATE verdicts on their teacher education schools. A few AFT locals have negotiated contracts that take professional rather than trade-unionist stances on important issues, such as dismissal of incompetent teachers and support for master teacher programs. On college and university campuses, student and peer judgments about professors' teaching effectiveness are becoming slightly more significant factors in promotion and tenure decisions. Even in the case of the hallowed tenure system, there are signs of incipient revolt. Younger faculty members who have been denied tenure—in a system that is often unfair and that devalues teaching—have been challenging the denial of their tenure in court and winning handsome settlements. The prospects for beneficial changes in these underlying structures are not bright, but neither are they hopeless.

Part Three

Prospects for
the Future

11

Who Really Wants Reform?
Who Will Pay?

Business leaders and working-class Americans have powerful reasons to support school reform. School bureaucracies, teacher unions, and the upper middle class still have their heads in the sand. Despite the lack of broad popular support, there are forces at work that will goad universities and schools into better performance, even without a popular uprising.

The prime motivating force behind the education-reform movement is the loss to foreign competitors of important markets for U.S.-manufactured goods. The spectre of a once-grand America slipping to Third World status has mobilized the energies of some of America's most powerful business, political, governmental, and union leaders. Our loss of "competitive edge" continues, and as long as it does, so will the school reform movement.

As the movement enters its second decade, we see that the current array of proposals is based on competing analyses of problems and on contradictory notions of what causes people and institutions to change. Despite the absence of a national consensus on which reforms to enact, all of the "second wave" reforms seem to

159

be based on deeper understanding of the complexities of American education. All reflect heightened awareness of the damage done by high-stakes, multiple-choice tests. There is widespread understanding that top-down mandates do not work very well unless they are accompanied by bottom-up renewal. Across the political spectrum, reformers seem to agree on at least one point: teachers know more than they are given credit for and should have a more powerful voice in decisions that affect their work.

When we count our national blessings, we should include the fact that so many smart people in business, politics, and education have stayed with the struggle long enough to lose their illusions and arrive at a deeper understanding of the complexities of reform. Foreign visitors to the United States are inspired by our cheerful and relentless efforts to keep working on the problem until we get it right.

Nevertheless, all "second wave" initiatives cost a lot of money, and governments at all levels are strapped. Moreover, few candidates for public office are willing to propose higher taxes, and those who do are not elected. Money is needed to induce arts and science academics to revamp curricula and improve teaching. Money is needed to attract and hold qualified teachers, provide them with classes small enough to make a difference, pay stipends to mentors, buy mentors time for observing and coaching inexperienced or ineffective teachers, and provide time for faculty members to work together on improving teaching and learning. Money is also needed to lengthen the school day and the school year, for the sake of students and teachers alike. In the inner cities, money is needed to keep children healthy enough to learn, house them when they are homeless, and, sometimes, keep the school's roof from literally falling on their heads. All of these are big-ticket items. Even "choice" plans, which seemed at first to involve merely the transfer of public funds from institutions to individuals, are turning out to be costly.

Does Business Really Mean It?

Prominent American corporate executives have been in the forefront of state and national educational reform efforts. For example, David T. Kearns, former chairman and CEO of Xerox Corporation and Assistant Secretary of Education under the Bush administration, and coauthor Denis P. Doyle argue for national standards and assessments of educational progress, slimmer educational bureaucracies, school choice, higher salaries for better-educated teachers, and year-round school, all of which, they claim, would promote teachers' autonomy and professionalism. They have also spoken up for larger federal outlays for educational research and full funding of Chapter I and Head Start.[1]

William S. Woodside, former chairman of the executive committee of Primerica Corporation, has promoted a vision of the future in which a better-educated work force will fill high-skills, high-wage jobs in an economy that depends more on brains than on brawn. Countless other American businesses participate in national, state, and local groups. Many corporations, with considerable fanfare, have donated truckloads of computers, offered scholarships to poor children, "adopted" local schools, and given their own employees time off to tutor children in nearby schools.

When it comes to coughing up money to support major reforms, or supporting tax increases, the corporate record looks impressive. For example, the Pew Charitable Trusts have given nearly $20 million to the Philadelphia Public Schools to support site-based management of schools. They have been loudly beating the drums for better schools, and because of their high status in American society, their drums have been heard, especially by wealthy Americans, who until recently have been unwilling to pay more taxes to support the schools.

The RJR Nabisco Corporation has contributed $30 million to support bottom-up reforms at individual schools. In Alabama, business groups have pushed for major tax increases for education. The radical restructuring of schools in Kentucky has been sustained by the business community. In Oklahoma, an election to repeal tax increases for education failed because of vigorous opposition from the business community.

These examples notwithstanding, the evidence suggests that some American business leaders are shedding crocodile tears over workers' deficiencies. Some advocate higher taxes, but only those taxes that the "little people" pay. Few are willing to pay more corporate property or income taxes, and some have contrived to pay no taxes at all. Here is what Robert Reich has to say:

> Despite the hoopla, corporate donations to education actually tapered off markedly in the 1980s. While in the 1970s corporate giving to education jumped an average of 15 percent a year, by the late 1980s it was climbing at a snail's pace. . . . And notably, most of it was allocated to colleges and universities—in particular, to the alma maters of symbolic analysts, where their children and grandchildren were likely to follow in their footsteps. Only 1.5 percent of corporate giving in 1989 was directed toward primary and secondary schools. . . . This tiny sum was, notably, smaller than the amounts received by corporations from states and locales in the form of subsidies and tax breaks quietly procured under threat that the corporation otherwise would move to a more congenial tax base. . . . The executives of General Motors, for example, who have been among the loudest to proclaim the need for better schools, have also been among the most relentless pursuers of local tax abatements. . . . All told, the corporate share of local tax revenues dropped from 45 percent in 1957 to around 16 percent in 1987. The newfound generosity of American-owned corporations toward America's less fortunate communities has been no match for the dramatic withdrawal of corporate tax revenues from the same localities.[2]

Jonathan Weisman, a reporter at the *San Jose Business Journal*, says that "skill shortages among high school graduates have virtually nothing to do with the dwindling competitiveness of the American work force. Rather, as an economic agenda, education is purely a smokescreen for inactivity." Weisman tells the story of the Fremont, California, auto plant that General Motors (GM) shut down ten years ago, claiming that the work force was impossible. When Toyota joined GM in a reopening of the plant, in 1984, the Japanese managers rehired 80 percent of the same workers, trained them in their specific jobs, managed them more intelligently, and made the plant the most productive in the GM galaxy. Moreover, says Weisman, "the United States will not need huge numbers of highly skilled workers in the future unless substantial changes are made in governmental policies and corporate practices." While Weisman acknowledges that the educational system needs an overhaul, it is not for the sake of high-skills, high-wage jobs, which hardly exist, but rather for the sake of kids in the inner cities, "whose schooling really is so woefully inadequate that they cannot hope to function in the American economy."[3]

In *Savage Inequalities,*[4] Jonathan Kozol writes about East St. Louis, which the U.S. Department of Housing and Urban Development describes as "the most distressed small city in America," and which the *St. Louis Post-Dispatch* has described as "America's Soweto." It is home to Monsanto, Big River Zinc, Cerro Copper, Aluminum Ore, the American Bottoms Sewage Plant and Trade Waste Incineration, and Pfizer. These industries have created small incorporated "towns," Sauget and Alorton, devices that have exempted them from paying taxes to support the schools or taking responsibility for the devastating health problems caused by the discharge of toxic wastes into the water, soil, and air of East St. Louis. Kozol quotes Safir Ahmed, a reporter from the *Post-Dispatch:*

> "Nobody in East St. Louis," Ahmed says, "has ever had the clout to raise a protest. Why Americans permit this is so hard for somebody like me, who grew up in the real Third World, to understand. . . .
>
> "I'm from India. In Calcutta this would be explicable, perhaps. I keep thinking to myself, 'My God! This is the United States!' "

There are no good generalizations about the role of business in educational reform. Some industrial leaders in some sectors see a need in the near future for better-trained workers to fill good-paying jobs, and those corporations are the ones in the forefront of advocacy and philanthropy. Most corporations and small businesses do not yet see the need for a better-educated work force. According to varying predictions, there will be only a modest increase over the next decade (from 5 percent to 15 percent) in jobs requiring post–high school education and training. Many corporations and small businesses are running on too thin a margin to consider supporting higher taxes, let alone donations. For many of them, the low-wage strategy is currently working.

But the low-wage strategy will fail eventually, just as the big-car and leveraged-buyout strategies failed. In the long run, in order to survive, the industrial leaders of the nation will have to invest in the development of the American people. In the meanwhile, we can count on some of America's most respected business leaders to beat the drums for reform, and they will be heard.

Do School Boards and Bureaucracies Want Change?

They say they do, and they plead piteously for higher teacher salaries, smaller classes, stipends for mentors, and money to train teachers and support the move toward school-site management and enactment of reforms. Urban superintendents complain about "the bureaucracy" as if it were the hand of God. For example, on June 10, 1992, the *Baltimore Sun* carried a story about a contract between the Baltimore City Schools and Education Alternatives, Inc. (EAI), a for-profit corporation traded on the NASDAQ over-the-counter exchange. EAI will run nine of the city's public schools on a five-year contract. Baltimore's superintendent said of this arrangement, "They can pierce the bureaucracy. There are many practices . . . that exist only to serve the bureaucracy, and our children fall between the cracks." The president of the Baltimore Teachers Union said, "We are very sorry that it takes the private sector to do this. We think it's something the public schools could easily have done, if not for the bureaucracy."[5]

Superintendents and their minions often talk as if they were powerless to change such practices as sending the worst and least experienced teachers to the schools with the most disadvantaged children. In 1988, the Council of Great City Schools, whose forty-five member districts enroll 12 percent of the nation's students and 30 percent of all minority students, reported that education graduates would rather teach anywhere except in the cities and deplored

the effects of high teacher turnover on the poorest student populations. "Eliminating other major obstacles to teacher retention,"
such as revising the seniority and "bumping" rights that allow
senior teachers the choicest teaching assignments, "may send shock
waves through the system," the report says.[6] Yet Albert Shanker,
president of the American Federation of Teachers, says that only 5
percent of teachers covered under union contracts are able to claim
"bumping" as a contractual right; it is usually a case of a bureaucracy's not being able to control itself, rather than a case of its being
controlled by a union.

No one familiar with the deplorable physical conditions in
inner-city schools, with overcrowded classrooms and book shortages, would deny that the schools need more money. But the man
on the street sees bloated state and local school bureaucracies—for
every teacher who is in a classroom in the United States, there is one
other school employee who is not—that do not seem willing to slim
down or stop themselves from making silly rules or get rid of
teachers who destroy children's desire to learn. They notice that all
those bureaucrats sometimes cannot even manage to get the books
to the schools on time.

The truculence of the taxpayers in the face of such obvious
need seems to be based on an unstated quid pro quo: "Consume a
little of your own fat before asking us to surrender more of ours."
As citizens become aware that many of the decisions formerly made
in central offices have been handed over to principals and teachers
in local schools, they will wonder more loudly why some of the
really serious needs cannot be paid for by a reduction in middle
management.

School board members find it very hard to eliminate the jobs
of the central office administrators who are usually looking them
in the eye during budget-cutting sessions. Superintendents find it
hard, too, because massive cuts in administration are demoralizing
to those who remain, and a demoralized organization is hard to run.
Nevertheless, it will be hard to coax taxpayers to pay more money
for the needed reforms unless there is evidence that managers have
demonstrated the same spirit of sacrifice that they expect of the
taxpaying citizens. Cincinnati's superintendent, J. Michael Brandt,
has read the tea leaves. He recently reduced the district's central

office and support staff by half and has liberated $16 million for local schools.[7]

Will University Leaders Pay
for Reforms in Teacher Education?

Probably not. The princes of the academy look with special favor on those departments that bring in big grants and contracts and cover the university with glory through published research, departments whose alumni are likely to make contributions to the alma mater. Departments of education do not contribute very much in any of these areas.

Even relatively low-cost enhancements of teacher education can be hard to pry loose from disdainful academics who control the purse. John Goodlad cites numerous examples of poisonous contempt for future teachers and those who teach them. One of them encapsulates my own observations: "A dean of humanities angrily and sarcastically denounced education professors but remained adamantly unwilling to devote any humanities resources to the teacher education program. He did not believe the education professors to be qualified to teach methods courses in the disciplines of the humanities, but he had no intention of 'lending' people in his division to do so."[8]

The schools of education are not entirely innocent in the matter, however. Most could eliminate or shorten some courses, especially those with meager intellectual content. Their apparent lack of resolve to get rid of the very aspects of teacher education that bring it into disrepute gives ammunition to their enemies, who then keep the enterprise in the universities' financial Twilight Zone.

There are some presidents and provosts who are putting time and money into better teacher education, but their numbers are small. For the moment, the social and financial incentives for university leaders to concern themselves with teacher education are very weak.

Will Teacher Unions Support Reform?

In the current antitax environment, teacher unions are not apt to give up their obsession with wages, hours, and working conditions—usually defined narrowly. If reform means longer hours, or any departure from the idea that every teacher is exactly as good as every other teacher, or any surrender of the principle of seniority, then most unions will not be willing to pay for reform at the moment.

At the national level, the American Federation of Teachers, through the powerful voice of its president, Albert Shanker, has sided with nearly every reform idea that leads to more professional roles for teachers. Shanker supports rigorous tests for licensure, periodic retesting of teachers, designated "professional development schools" for the training of beginning teachers, performance-based pay for master teachers, school choice for parents and students (within the public sector), and the granting of waivers from contractual provisions to schools that want to innovate and experiment. Shanker has even endorsed alternative certification. Not many local AFT affiliates have embraced Shanker's ideas, however. At the level of the school districts, it is generally difficult to discern any difference between an NEA affiliate and an AFT affiliate.

Will the Upper Middle Class Support and Pay for Reform?

Not at the moment, it seems. The system as it is almost guarantees that only the brightest students, or those with some combination of modest intellectual ability and favorable circumstances, will be able to put together the bits and pieces of the fragmented curriculum that characterizes most schools, even in affluent communities. And when the children of the affluent do not learn the fundamentals in this impoverished approach to teaching and learning, their parents can often boost their children's competitive advantage by enrolling them in coaching schools. Many upper-middle-class parents understand that today's norm-referenced tests pit students against each other, rather than against some objective standard. Competitive advantage for choice colleges, not learning, is understood to be the point of the game. Many such parents are content if their children merely score better than others, even if better is mediocre by the rest of the world's standards.

Theodore Sizer, founder and director of the Coalition of Essential Schools, works to expand the network of high schools dedicated to a deeper, richer education "where the kids really have to perform rather than go through the motions." Sizer finds that "the incentives for serious change are weak, particularly in schools serving the moderately affluent and affluent." Parents in such schools, he says, often resist change efforts: "The school doesn't need fixing; the kids get into Stanford and Brown—don't change a thing."[9]

Either affluent parents have cynically accepted the need to play the test-score game or they do not really understand what the tests are like. Sizer asks parents to shadow a student for a day or two.

"Very few adults, particularly those who are older, remember what it's like to go seven consecutive periods studying subjects in isolation. They don't remember how boring it is and how much of it is intellectually incoherent," he says. Sizer also tries to persuade parents to accept change by showing them the tests: "Do you ever bother to look at the tests? No? Please look at these tests. Do the 'right' or 'wrong' answers on this test satisfy you as an indicator of your child's performance, or as something with which to make judgments about your child?" When parents do look, they "go into orbit," Sizer says. He thinks that the most powerful incentives for change would be a sense of higher standards inside each family, but "governmental or national commissions are not going to give families those incentives or those beliefs." He takes the long view: "We need places to bear witness that poor kids can learn . . . and we're beginning to see those kinds of results in Coalition schools serving low-income populations."

There are upper-middle-class parents who know that their children are not getting a good public education, and whose solution is not to push for reform but to send their children to private schools and lobby for voucher plans. John Kenneth Galbraith lays out the political dynamics of this movement:

> Whereas the poor have no alternative to the public schools, the more fortunate pay separately, in fact, for their own. These are either the better-financed public schools of the more affluent suburbs or private schools. In the latter case, the fortunate have to pay twice, and one of their more plausible reactions is the

suggestion that they should be remitted the equivalent of the taxes they pay for public education in a voucher usable for private schools of their choice. Thus they would escape the burden of the double educational cost. By convention, however, this is not put so rudely: freedom of choice, liberty, the wise privatization of public activity—these are the most frequently heard justifications.[10]

Will Working-Class Americans Support Reform?

If the upper middle class is currently satisfied with the schools, what about working-class Americans? Are they satisfied, even though the evidence suggests that their kids are not being given a fair shake? Inexplicably, public opinion polls say that most Americans like their local schools, even if they think the schools in general are not very good.

But polls are blunt instruments, and there are signs that schools serving poor and working-class families are more willing to change. According to Sizer, those communities are more receptive than affluent communities to the approach of the Coalition of Essential Schools. One reason for this greater receptivity may be that the working class is getting firsthand experience with the consequences of poor education. Among the ten million unemployed Americans in 1992 are many older workers who were laid off because they lacked the math and literacy skills to work in modern plants and mills or even to be retrained for other jobs. Their adult children are more likely to be living with them, either because their minimum-wage jobs do not allow them to live independently or because they cannot find work at all. For example, when Howard LeHuquet, a forty-eight-year-old blast-furnace worker, lost his $35,000-per-year job, he thought he might train himself for either computer repair or air conditioning and heating work, but he failed the math test required for admission to either program: "Now why do you need so much math to get down and fix an air conditioner or a refrigerator? I was working all these years, paying the bills, paying off this house, making car payments. You don't realize time goes by and then, *bang!* It's gone. Everything is math."[11] LeHuquet's three children still live at home. One is still in school, but the two who have graduated cannot earn enough to move out. LeHuquet and millions like him are painfully learning that academic skills matter, and that the schools are often failing to teach their children what they need to know in a modern workplace. If the choice is between bread and algebra, they may not be willing to pay more taxes, but they will probably have more and more to say about the quality of their children's education than in the past.

Goads, Portents, and Straws in the Wind

Despite the generally weak popular support for serious school reform, there are forces at work that may push the educational system into better performance and provide more support for teachers as they struggle to serve a population of children that is less well looked after than those in previous generations.

National Standards, National Assessment

In 1989, President Bush and the nation's governors set in motion a series of events that led to the formation of the National Educational Goals Panel (NEGP). Lauren Resnick of the Learning Resource and Development Center at the University of Pittsburgh, and author of *Education and Learning to Think,* and Mark Tucker, president of the National Center on Education and the Economy, who wrote *America's Choice: High Skills or Low Wages,* worked on NEGP and launched the New Standards Project in 1991, a result in part of their work with NEGP. The project had been conceived several years earlier, when they fell to talking about the links between their ideas. They concluded that if we want a good economy, we need good thinkers and good assessment in turn, since what we test is what we value. Tucker and Resnick's work on NEGP accelerated the progess of their own plans and was the final push needed to give birth to the New Standards Project. The project is aimed at achieving consensus among the cooperating partners (seventeen states and six districts, at last count) on what students should know and be able to do, and at creating a national assessment system (not a single national test) that will measure students' progress toward the national standards.

Advocates of national standards and assessment talk as if the virtues of national standards and examinations were self-evident, as if the mere setting of high standards helps people achieve them, and as if examinations will make everybody work harder. Perhaps so. David W. Hornbeck, former Maryland state superintendent of schools, has made a more explicit case for national standards and exams: "The single greatest obstacle faced by poor and minority students is the low expectations most adults have for their performance. Expectations are powerful, self-fulfilling prophecies. A highly visible national process of creating high standards and a rigorous examination system would create expectations for disadvantaged students that are now lower than those held for others."[12]

It could be added that low expectations are a problem in every community for the great majority of students, poor or not, minority or majority. Parents are complacent. Moreover, local school officials tailor their expectations to what they see as unbeatable social forces—broken homes, drugs, guns, health problems, language deficiencies, uncaring parents—and think that they are doing as well as can be expected under the circumstances. National standards could be a wake-up call for parents and local school officials. Everybody would have an external, objective point of reference for judging whether kids are really being prepared for the world as it is and is becoming.

Many oppose national standards and exams, however, and for cogent reasons. Even if there were a critical mass of supporters, creating national standards and tests is frighteningly expensive. And if Congress appropriates the money to build the system, it will cost local school systems a lot more money to grade more complex assessments, such as essays and science demonstrations.

Whatever the political fate of the national-standards movement, and whether or not there are improved national assessments, the national conversation on a subject that was taboo only a decade ago is a goad to teachers and public school officials, who must now think harder about ways to improve students' performance.

Many states are also going ahead on their own to define standards and encourage better teaching through more sophisticated tests of students' understanding. The National Assessment of Educational Progress (NAEP), which has been testing a small sample of American students in all academic areas for many years, is moving toward the kinds of tests that will require teachers to teach for understanding, rather than for soon-to-be-forgotten details.

Choice Plans

There is also a national conversation going on about choice. Choice plans that provide tuition vouchers to all parents who want to send their children to private or parochial schools are bitterly opposed by supporters of the public schools. Tuition vouchers for low-income students are less often opposed. In either case, however, permitting vouchers to be spent on religious schools raises difficult constitutional issues. Whatever the legal and political fate of public-private voucher plans, the fact that leaders continue to propose them keeps the pressure on the public schools to justify both their expenditures and their results.

Even the more popular choice plans, which allow the student to attend any public school, are a goad to the public schools. But whether the goad of competition leads to higher standards, as advocates claim, is highly debatable. Anecdotal evidence suggests that public school choice plans are as likely to lower standards as to raise them. Some parents transfer their adolescents to schools with easier grading policies, on the theory that a higher grade-point average ensures admission to a better college. In the more typical case, students with special interests in music or sports transfer to schools with spectacular band directors or football coaches. Sometimes the competitive response of the school that is losing students is not what choice advocates have in mind. For example, in order to stanch the outflow of musicians or wide receivers, a high school may beef up its music or sports program, but these program improvements inevitably come at the expense of the academic program, since school budgeting is a zero-sum game.

In places where parents and students can choose from among public schools, there seems to be a trend toward the "fast-food phenomenon": when one fast-food chain offers fish sticks or tacos or a salad bar, then the others follow suit; everybody eventually offers everything, and nothing is done very well. Whether choice plans are good or bad for education, and whether competition among schools drives standards up or down, the current political rhetoric is not helping people understand the issues. A more honest national debate could clarify the issues and prod public schools to justify their virtual monopoly.

"Alternate Route" Plans

Even if many "alternate route" plans involve little more than sugar-coated emergency licensing, the fact that such plans have been legitimized in most of the fifty states is a new turn in American education. To the extent that people can be trained to be good teachers, with fewer formal courses and more direct experience, the schools of education will be kept under pressure to figure out more efficient ways of doing things.

NCATE

NCATE is not yet a giant stalking the landscape, but it is getting bigger and stronger. If for no other reason than professional pride, many faculties in schools of education would like to meet NCATE's new and higher standards and are energized by the effort to meet them. Even if NCATE's current criteria for accreditation are not the final word, it is certain that NCATE will continue to refine its process and isolate the most crucial factors in good teacher preparation. The ultimate test of the NCATE system will be whether employing school districts, students, and parents can see any distinguishing characteristics in a graduate of an NCATE-approved school of education, and whether the states have the political will to abide by the verdict that a particular school of education is not able to produce qualified teachers.

The National Board for Professional Teaching Standards (NBPTS)

NBPTS is defining standards for highly accomplished teachers, not beginners. The standards will encompass not only teaching skills and knowledge of students, in all their variety, but also the depth of a teacher's subject matter knowledge and his or her ability to translate it for students at various stages of development. If, as expected, states decide to reward NBPTS-certified teachers with higher pay and give them responsibility for the training of other teachers, NBPTS would have an enormous impact on the education and training of teachers. If large numbers of the graduates of particular institutions failed content knowledge tests or failed to demonstrate highly accomplished teaching, then those institutions would be goaded to improve their programs. Similarly, if the working conditions in particular school districts prevented teachers from acquiring the skills required for NBPTS certification, then NBPTS could have a positive impact on the way school districts treat their teachers.

NBPTS certification promises to cut through a problem that has plagued teaching and schooling for many decades: the public is willing to pay more money for *better* teachers, but not for *all* teachers. Local school districts lack the talent and money to develop systems for identifying "better" teachers, at least systems that the great mass of teachers would respect. NBPTS does have the resources to develop a sophisticated, content-specific, culturally sensitive way of deciding who is "better." The crucial test for NBPTS will be whether those who earn National Board certification are seen by their peers and by the public as worthy of their rank and deserving of higher pay. If NBPTS certification passes the test, then the long, bitter battle over differentiated pay may finally end.

The New American Schools
Development Corporation (NASDC)

Part of President Bush's educational initiative, the America 2000 program, was the creation of a nonprofit, privately funded corporation (NASDC) to organize competition for innovative ideas about "break-the-mold" schools that could bring their students up to "world-class standards." Bush expected American businesses to donate $200 million over the course of six years to support the project. So far, $50 million—a full quarter—has been pledged. Despite a certain amount of cynicism about the rhetoric, the lure of money and the challenge of coming up with new ideas stimulated about 800 proposals. After an initial screening, NASDC's panels of proposal readers considered 686 new designs for schools. In July of 1992, NASDC awarded grants to eleven design teams.

It will be years before anyone knows whether NASDC schools will outperform ordinary schools, or whether the good ideas that come out of the project will have any impact on schooling in general. But the experiment will be closely watched. In the end, it may provide the system with some fresh inspiration, especially if the Clinton administration gives its support, as it is expected to do.

Renewed Interest in Family Policy

The disintegration of families and the poor condition of so many of the nation's children has led to a spate of proposals and programs designed to promote family stability and alleviate the poverty and malnutrition that are the fate of about one-fifth of our children. There are moves to expand early childhood education, to provide health care to children whose parents cannot afford it, and to organize a national system to track down fathers who will not support their children. Although nobody knows how to do it yet, lots of people are trying to figure out how to reduce teen pregnancies, drug abuse, and street violence. The recognition of the deplorable circumstances of millions of American children is a hopeful straw in the wind.

The reform of teacher education and of education in general is not yet an urgent priority. The most powerful entities in our society are willing to advocate change but are less willing to spend time penetrating the complexities of the task or to spend money on such an uncertain venture. But it is also true that yesterday's heresies are becoming the promising new programs—or, at least, the subjects of a respectable national argument.

12

The "Velvet Revolution"— Teachers as Reformers

Teachers are more pained than anyone else by our out-moded, self-deceiving system of public education. Collectively, they know better than the rest of us what needs to be changed if we are to meet national goals for the education of all children and improve the training of incoming teachers. Sooner or later, there will be a critical mass of teachers with the courage to change the system.

There are moments of joy in teaching. Such a moment arrives when a teacher who has spent days or weeks trying to get a difficult concept across "sees the lights go on," as teachers often describe it. The lights are in the eyes of the students who suddenly understand—when what was dimly seen before suddenly becomes bright, and when they see the connections between one thing and another.

Teachers of art, music, and drama know moments of joy unknown to teachers of academic subjects. Breakthroughs in these arts require students to go beyond the mastery of verbal knowledge and into the deeper realms of self. The onerous discipline of technical mastery and daily practice is hard enough. The art student must also risk exposure of his soul. The music student must draw

176

from his entire being and then submerge it into an ensemble. The drama student must put himself into the heart and soul of the character and at the same time be true to himself. To help a student find this difficult balance of outer discipline and inner freedom and truth is to know a deep satisfaction.

Athletic coaches have their own special joys. Good ones are masters at analyzing their students' capacities and coaching them toward higher levels. Coaches help their students discover the fruits of dedication and self-discipline. They lead their students to a reconciliation between brute force and strategy, between risk taking and prudence, between solitary glory and teamwork. Like all other teachers, they help their students cope with the consequences of success and failure. In the case of sports, however, those consequences are more severe because they are more public. Coaches enjoy the public's adulation when their teams win trophies, but that pleasure pales by comparison with the private joy of seeing a girl or a boy learn the more subtle and long-lasting lessons that athletic competition can teach.

Special-education teachers know joy when a mute child says his first words, when a blind child makes contact with the printed word, when a retarded child reads well enough to get around the world on his own, when a disturbed child discovers she can surmount her problems, and when a teenager slated for a lifetime of dependency lands a simple job. The world will little note nor long remember what those special-education teachers did in reconverted broom closets or cinder-block cubes. But society is nevertheless indebted to their insight and dedication and their deep knowledge of how to penetrate the barriers to learning.

Teaching can bring Zenlike raptures, as when waves of thought and response wash back and forth between teacher and students, when all have momentarily lost self-consciousness and are unified in a symphonic effort to figure something out or create something. Lots of teachers work late into the night, planning lessons they hope will be gems. When the lesson connects with the students, it is like hitting a tennis ball in the middle of the racquet and hearing that satisfying "whock," or pulling a perfect cake out of the oven, or clinching a profitable deal—only better.

The things that teachers learn from those moments are, by

perverse tradition, locked up inside their individual heads and class-rooms. Faculty meetings are from 3:15 to 4:05 on Thursdays, and the principal usually talks the whole time. Teachers who have produced "whocks" during the week are not invited to speak. An unwritten rule in the dysfunctional American school culture is that teachers should report neither their successes nor their failures to others—certainly not the failures. Even where the rule is being broken, there is seldom a time or place where teachers can talk seriously to one another about their work and learn from one another.

At in-service workshops, the experts talk the whole time. The presumptions of the in-service training tradition are that non-teachers can "fix" deficient teachers by talking at them and that teachers have nothing of value to contribute to the topic at hand. The teacher who has figured out how to teach latitude and longitude so that the kids have the concept in their bones, or who has found the way to make *Wuthering Heights* relevant to Hispanic teenagers in Los Angeles, is not invited to speak. Nevertheless, these private discoveries and clandestine victories are the things that keep teachers going in spite of the dispiriting conditions under which most of them work.

There are other and more subtle satisfactions in teaching, mostly unknown to outsiders and sometimes unrecognized by teachers themselves. In the world outside the schools, adults are protected from any knowledge of their little hypocrisies, pompos-ities, and self-deceptions by the politeness of other adults. Teachers, however, spend their days with young people who are not only experts at spotting the foibles of adults but also fresh enough to comment on them. Teachers who spend their lives experiencing the audible scrutiny of their students come to know themselves better than most other adults do. As La Rochefoucauld said, "It is as easy to deceive oneself without perceiving it as it is difficult to deceive others without their perceiving it."[1] Because kids are harder to fool than adults, teaching is a lifelong education in the self and in the near-impossibility of deceiving others.

Teachers and school principals also have a front-row seat in the great cultural theater of the United States. They know about the arrival of new immigrant groups and are the first to discover the details of how their cultures converge or conflict with mainstream American culture. They are the first to know when the factory shuts down, when parents lose their jobs, and when families are evicted—because parents come in to fill out free-lunch forms. School people usually know why families move in and move out of neighborhoods, and where they came from and where they are going—because school records follow children around the country. School people are the first to know about epidemics—because they talk to the parents of kids who are absent. They know when there are small shifts in the code of the teenage peer group, or in the popular culture. The rest of us usually learn of such things later, after the scholars have gathered the data and crunched the numbers, and after the journalists have written the stories.

Adults who do not work in schools tend to think that principals and teachers are not in the "real world" because they do not have to meet a payroll and cannot be fired at the drop of a hat. Ironically, school people also tend to think that the world outside is the "real world," and that theirs is not. But the real world makes itself known to principals and teachers in gritty ways that elude business, government, or professional workers. If there is satisfaction in knowing how the great American experiment is unfolding, those who work in schools have a large measure of that satisfaction.

Liberating Teachers' Intelligence
at Gavin Elementary School

The isolation of teachers from one another and from the adult working world, along with the world's lack of interest in what teachers know, is fatiguing. Margo Street, a teacher at Gavin Elementary School in Chicago Heights, began teaching primary students with enthusiasm. As the years went by, however, "she began to feel tired, ineffectual, and finally burned out."[2]

> It seemed that I was trying, but I wasn't getting any-place. I moved from primary because I wanted to see what the problem was with older children. . . . I switched to sixth grade. For a couple of years that was fine, because it was a different type of teaching. Then

about five years ago I grew very tired. It seemed I was
at a standstill. The faculty was not as supportive of
each other. We had gone through severe changes in
the community, which had always been a low socio-
economic community.

Margo Street got a new lease on life when her principal,
Yvonne Robinson, heard about the Accelerated Schools Project
from an assistant superintendent, Barbara Gore. The model is designed to bring at-risk children up to mainstream standards by sixth
grade. It requires principals to stop thinking of themselves as
branch managers and start thinking of ways to draw on the faculty's
strengths. Gore knew that the plan would fail unless at least 75
percent of the teachers supported it, and so Robinson took her time,
letting the faculty absorb the new ideas and vent their anxieties
about them. Finally, the frustrated faculty gave its overwhelming
approval to giving it a try.

The first step in reconstructing the school required the
teachers to engage in the painful and foreign process of discussing
their strengths and weaknesses openly. Jackie McFarland, a twenty-
one-year veteran at Gavin who saw her strength in science and chose
to specialize in it under the reform plan, reported the results:

Since everybody chose their strengths, they love what
they're doing. There is a different attitude now. Before, teachers would go in, close the door, and say they
were in their private world. Now, we meet on a weekly
basis and try to connect the curriculum so science
won't seem so isolated from math and math won't
seem so isolated from social studies. When the attitude
of the teachers changed, the attitude of the kids
changed.[3]

Although the kids used to hate state achievement tests,
"Pretty soon we could hear their voices calling out: 'I *know* this!
We've had this! We studied this . . . this is *easy*. We can *do* this,'"
McFarland reports.

Before McFarland was given the freedom to teach for understanding, as well as the responsibility for deciding how to do that, she thought she had to make the kids read a certain amount of material, whether they understood it or not. Now she sets up science experiments so that kids learn the concepts before they read the textbooks. For example, she organized a demonstration to help her students discover for themselves the answer to the question "Can air rise?" The kids stacked tables and blew air into Ziploc bags wedged between the tables. When the tables rose, the kids laughed and screamed, but they got hold of the concept. In many American schools, her homegrown experiment would have brought down the wrath of the principal because the class would have been seen as out of control.

The Power of Central Park East Secondary School (CPESS)

The power of restructuring with a purpose is displayed in East Harlem, where the students at Central Park East Secondary School (80 percent of whom qualify for free lunch) are making academic history—completing high school, getting into colleges. Teachers are working in teams, not only to plan a coherent, integrated curriculum but also to create a familial atmosphere. Interns are learning to be great beginning teachers, because they are in a great school and are mentored by great teachers. Despite its stunning successes with students, CPESS still has to fight endless battles with the infamous New York City Public Schools bureaucracy just to keep on doing what it is doing.

Herb Rosenfeld, codirector of CPESS, taught for eighteen years at New York City's prestigious Bronx High School of Science, but traditional teaching wore him out, even in a school with highly motivated, high-achieving students:

> I felt tired. I was an energetic guy with a lot of stamina, but the fifth class of the day never got what the third class got. I taught advanced classes, I did experimental work, I did things that were reserved for stars to do, but I was still tired. I think that most teachers are really dissatisfied. The difficulty is getting them to

see that this kind of change really deals with the dissatisfaction.

The dissatisfaction of so many teachers with their isolation, and with their lack of control over their own work, is reflected in the 1991 Metropolitan Life Survey of the American Teacher. When asked what changes would be most helpful in being a more effective teacher, 21 percent of experienced teachers said they wanted more opportunities to work cooperatively with other teachers, to enhance each other's skills. A 1990 poll conducted by the Carnegie Foundation for the Advancement of Teaching showed that 75 percent of the teachers surveyed were dissatisfied with the degree of control they had over their work, as compared to 55 percent only three years earlier.[4] Those figures do not yet suggest a national mandate for restructuring, but they do suggest a trend that seems to be building on itself. As teachers hear more about other teachers who have a voice in setting policies for student retention and promotion and shaping curriculum, or who have a voice in the selection of their own colleagues, they become more frustrated with their isolation and with the curricular and testing policies that drag the whole enterprise down, as well as with the fact that they do not even have much choice over the most essential tools of their craft—instructional materials for their students.

The Rocky Road to Collaborative Decision Making

The restructuring movement's purpose is to advance learning for everyone in the schools. The idea behind moving decisions from state and local bureaucracies to the school site is to capture teachers' knowledge of particular students and their needs. But as teachers have been given official permission to make important decisions, it has become evident that a change in governance does not automatically lead to better results. The transition from obedient clerk to empowered professional is slow and difficult.

Teachers have been conditioned to want what their unions fight for—more pay, shorter hours, smaller classes. Under school-site management, they are suddenly supposed to want other things—higher standards for students, better teaching, longer working hours (in order to collaborate), and more responsibility for running the schools. Integral to school-site management and to school-based teacher education is the idea that some teachers are better than others. That idea cuts against the grain of trade-unionist solidarity and equality, and against the tradition that makes sharp distinctions between teachers and administrators. Teachers are expected to invest their hearts in a grueling process, on the gamble that somewhere down the road they will be happier even if they are working harder.

David T. Conley has studied schools in Oregon that are traveling the rocky road to restructuring and has pinpointed the pitfalls. Some faculties tinker at the margins and lack a coherent vision. Some "get sidetracked on one issue and spend most of their time spinning their wheels trying to resolve it." Some ignore their communities and later discover, to their regret, strong community resistance to change. Some have only a superficial understanding of what it means to restructure. Many look at trivial changes through rose-colored glasses and call them restructuring. Many faculties, as well as their superiors in central offices, think that a change in governance is an end in itself. Nearly everybody is trying to measure new kinds of learning with tools (standardized tests) that do not capture essential and deep understanding of content, let alone the ability to make connections among disciplines. "Analysis paralysis" is, according to Conley, "one of the striking features of the current interest in school restructuring." The faculty studies the situation to death and keeps on doing what it was doing before. Finally, Conley says, schools tend to isolate the innovators in one wing or program area, making no commitment to changing the total program on the basis of what the innovators learn.[5]

Getting past all these pitfalls is a necessary part of reforming teacher education. As we have seen in previous chapters, even the best-educated, best-trained teachers may be brought down to the least common denominator in teaching if they train in schools that are not geared up to show them what good teaching looks like and how a truly effective faculty works.

The beginning teacher needs to complete training in a successful public school where the community of teachers and parents has signed on to a coherent vision of what schools are for—where learning to teach is understood to be a collegial activity, and where the ethos of the faculty supports a continuous and undefensive effort to learn from one's successes and failures with students.

What stands in the way of that kind of on-the-job training are old, hierarchical assumptions; the enshrinement of low expectations in laws, mandates, curricula, tests, and textbooks; the unwillingness of many principals to surrender the power they have been exercising badly; the shopworn attitudes of many union leaders; and the fact that most teachers would rather submit to the current system than fight it.

A Change in Management Style Is Inevitable

There are forces in motion that will erode most of these barriers over the next few years. In business and industry, the old hierarchical organizations are losing ground to "flatter," more democratic organizations that involve workers more in decisions about how to make a business more profitable. In the most successful businesses, accountability is achieved through the power of groups of workers to achieve goals, not through legions of middle managers who are handsomely paid to make rules and supervise workers.

In 1989, at a "Tomorrow's Schools" seminar at Michigan State University, Tom Skrtic of Kansas said:

> The most optimistic thing I see going on is that bureaucracy will not be the dominant choice in the next political economy. It will be "adhocracy" because the days when we can make large runs of standardized products are over. The postindustrial economy ultimately will shape our schools as "adhocracies". . . . You can't have a political, professional form of accountability in a bureaucracy because of the isolation. You can't have an ongoing dialogue amongst teams of professionals because they're all locked away in little rooms. Schools of education are the same sort of configuration. The very structure of the organization prevents us from instituting the forms of accountability

that would do better than the ways that are logic[al]
for bureaucracy. [6]

Most school superintendents and principals are still wedded
to patriarchal notions of leadership, but some are beginning to
learn that teachers are experts on certain matters and should be
partners rather than subordinates in the running of schools. Some
are learning that distributing power, rather than hoarding it, is a
better way to improve a school's performance.

In most contemporary degree programs for school administrators, aspiring principals are learning the management principles
of successful businesses and industries. They are being trained to be
hero makers rather than heroes, to be moral rather than technocratic
leaders. Thomas J. Sergiovanni of Trinity University in San Antonio not only trains future administrators to be new-style leaders but
also trains teacher education students for the leadership roles they
will play in the future, even if they remain classroom teachers.
Instead of the "command" model of school leadership, where principals exhaust themselves trying to control people according to bu-
reacratic rules, Sergiovanni proposes a new type of school
leadership, more suited to the communal, familial, and professional
character of schools. In such a setting, "teachers with special insights into teaching share them with others; they do not define
success in terms of what happens in their own classrooms when the
school itself may be failing."[7] He elaborates:

> Improving schools is difficult because we give too
> much attention to direct leadership. We focus almost
> exclusively on leadership as something forceful, di-
> rect, and interpersonal, instead of paying at least
> equal attention to providing substitutes for leader-
> ship. The more successful we are in providing these
> substitutes, the more likely it is that teachers and oth-
> ers will become self-managing. Principals will be able
> to spend more time on issues of substance than [on]
> process. [8]

Instead of the boss-employee relationship, whereby principals and supervisors, "by virtue of their rank, are presumed to know

more than teachers and staff," Sergiovanni sees the principal as a principal *teacher,* as someone who is deeply interested in the details of teaching and learning and who promotes accountability through the authentic expression of disappointment or, if necessary, of outrage. According to Sergiovanni, "Nobody has a special license to protect the standard. The only thing that makes the leader special is that she or he is a better follower: better at articulating the purposes of the community, more passionate about them, more willing to take time to pursue them."[9]

The new-style principal, backed up by national standards and examinations and by professional norms, is the key to the reform of teacher education and teaching. Through cultural leadership, rather than bureaucratic control, the proper climate for expert teaching and the induction of new teachers will be established. Through professional and moral leadership, rather than technical leadership, principals will become the necessary "check and balance" against the low expectations, fuzzy ideas, triviality, impersonality, and absence of clear purpose that now plague American education. In the near future, as the old-style authoritarian superintendents, supervisors, and principals retire and are replaced by superiors whose conceptions of leadership are uniquely fitted to schooling, the picture will begin to change.

A Change in Union Philosophy Is Inevitable

Most local union leaders are still in an adversarial mode, tightly focused on wages and grievances. Most union leaders will resist any plan to differentiate one teacher from another, especially if there is money attached to the differentiation. Many still think that the shift of authority to the school level is a management trick to undercut the union's power.

This shift of authority is not a trick to undermine unions; it is a plan to improve teaching and learning. But most union leaders oppose attempts to expand teachers' jobs into quasi-managerial roles. For the same reason, many school administrators and administrator unions are also opposed to any change that threatens to usurp their managerial power, as they currently understand that power.

Teacher unions will change, however, whether they want to or not. Rank-and-file teachers are beginning to define accomplished practice in their own language, not in the language of teacher educators, educational researchers, school bureaucracies, or the textbook publishers. As teachers learn to talk and write about what they *do,* they are beginning to know what they *know* and to learn that they have much to contribute to other teachers. This first step in real restructuring—teachers' knowing what they know—is crucial. From there, the creation of energized, self-propelling schools depends on two other crucial conditions: designation of expert teachers to take on quasi-supervisory roles within the school, and provision of time for teachers to work together on the details of teaching and learning.

At the moment, the effort to create a cadre of leaders within the teaching ranks is rhetorically supported by nearly everybody and actually supported by very few. Even when union leaders make approving sounds about "career ladders" and other forms of performance-based pay, they often obstruct programs to differentiate teachers according to merit by nitpicking over the details of the plans. Administrators who publicly support restructuring often resist at the level of details. For example, the teachers in a "collaborative decision-making school" may discover that the principal has selected the textbooks all by himself. Administrators in central offices see the handwriting on the wall: as more decisions are moved to teachers in local schools, their jobs and higher salaries are harder to justify.

The provision of time is problematic. Teachers may be willing to work extra hours without pay for a few months or an academic year, but sooner or later they will tire of putting out effort for a project that the school district does not value enough to pay for. School boards are under pressure to cut budgets, and school bashers will be quick to characterize teachers' work sessions as unnecessary blather.

Where paid time and enlightened leadership do exist, however, teachers are beginning to experience relief from their isolation, as well as the joy of being more successful with students while trading secrets with other teachers. Those who are taking on added responsibilities are beginning to believe that they should indeed be paid more than other teachers. To the extent that their desires are thwarted by their own unions, the unions will be undermined—not because school restructuring is a cunning trick, but because of teachers' growing professionalism. To the extent that teachers are thwarted by administrators who are fighting a last-ditch effort to maintain the old dysfunctional system, management will be undermined—it will soon become apparent that students do better if their teachers are not systematically stripped of their sense of personal responsibility. (That sense of personal responsibility is what gives most teachers in private schools their edge, even when they are no better educated or trained than public school teachers.)

The Metropolitan Life Survey of the American Teacher shows that a slight majority of teachers now supports some form of performance-based pay, favors tests for incoming teachers, and thinks that talented people without conventional credentials could improve the schools. The unions will not be far behind or else they will lose members.

The unions are already responding, in fact. The American Federation of Teachers has supported, at least at the national level, the restructuring movement. For eleven years, the AFT has sponsored a project that presents research findings about teaching and learning to its members. The AFT's Dale Boatwright, who works with teachers around the nation in the Educational Research and Dissemination Project, believes that the study of significant research is an effective way of bringing teachers' tacit knowledge to the surface—the first crucial step in meaningful restructuring.

Two local AFT affiliates, in Toledo and Cincinnati, are doing what the public has always said teachers should do—taking responsibility for cleaning their own houses. Both local unions run teacher evaluation systems far more sophisticated than the superficial checklist approach that prevails in virtually all management-dominated school systems. These affiliates select and deploy expert teachers who coach poor teachers and collaborate in the dismissal of those who do not respond to the coaching.

The National Education Association runs the Mastery In Learning Project, which fosters rethinking of schooling and teaching in member schools. Through a computer hookup, teachers in participating schools can call up information on issues they are studying and communicate with teachers in other network schools.

In Miami, Rochester, Chicago, and the entire state of Kentucky, school-site management, coupled with the direct involvement of teachers in consequential decisions, is already a reality. In most of the schools in Philadelphia, and in hundreds of individual pilot projects in schools across the nation, teachers are beginning to trust one another and to receive mutual critiques in good spirit. Scenes such as these give signs that there will come a time, in the not too distant future, when teachers are sure enough of their own special expertise and articulate enough to justify their positions to policy makers and the public.

The Composition of the Teaching Force Will Change

How do these predictions of inevitable change tally with what was said earlier about the passivity of so many young people in today's education programs and their easy submission to the status quo in the schools where they teach? The composition of the teaching force over the next decade will inevitably change because the standards for entering the profession are rising and because the population is changing.

Teacher shortages in the 1960s and 1970s gave rise to the "any warm body" approach to filling vacancies. Semiliterate teachers were given licenses and tenure, but those teachers are now approaching retirement, and a better-educated group of teachers is entering the system. The emergence of so many postbaccalaureate education programs is attracting older adults, who have known success in other endeavors and are therefore more self-confident: career switchers, retired military personnel, and people who have lost middle-management jobs as businesses have gotten leaner. "Alternate route" programs are drawing a higher proportion of African-Americans, Hispanics, Asians, and other minorities, who will be more passionately concerned with proper education of minority kids and more willing to challenge the system that has failed them. Programs like Teach for America are drawing in a scattering of highly educated young people from elite colleges, who may not stay long but will have a powerful influence nevertheless.

Jerry Rosiek, who graduated from Texas A&M University with a degree in physics and philosophy, became a high school teacher in an impoverished Mexican-American community in Texas through an "alternate route" program. In 1990, after two years of teaching, he had this to say:

> Alternatively certified teachers are a renewable resource, replenished each year by frustrated graduates. The option to walk away from teaching gives these teachers an important asset: the personal freedom to confront an oppressive and dysfunctional administration bent on self-preservation. . . . This last point is worth considering. If one of the obstructions to our perennial attempts at reform is an entrenched education bureaucracy, then people not beholden to it must infiltrate it and overthrow it. Alternative certification is our best source of the subversives needed in any future attempt to reform education. Moreover, I think they should be trained as such [subversives].[10]

Even a decade ago, such a piece would not have been written, let alone printed in to the *New York Times*. The mere existence of Rosiek's commentary shows that the evolution of teaching into a profession is already happening. Otherwise, the restructuring movement and the move to school-site governance would not be underway. Those who have traditionally exercised control, or the illusion of control, would not now be handing some of it over to teachers unless they had reason to think that it was in their best interests to do so.

There are now, as always, myriad little streams of discontent running through the teaching population of the United States, and it is easy to find teachers who are cynical and angry. A major source of teachers' discontent is the conflict they feel between doing what they think is best for their students and doing what they are usually told to do by their superiors—get the test scores up. In a personal communication about his life as an educational researcher and reformer, Arthur Wise had this to say: "If teachers follow mandated policies, they worry that they are shortchanging their students, even if the students perform better on the standardized tests. As a result of this ethical conflict, many teachers leave the field or adopt coping strategies designed to meet the letter of the law. But teachers continue to feel guilty because they know that, as test scores rise, the quality of education is deteriorating."

On top of the ethical conflict is the enduring humiliation of not being taken seriously. Persistent indignity causes some teachers to become lazy or ill-tempered time servers who teach by the book and work to the rule. Others take refuge in fanaticism or other energizing forms of defiance. It is the presence of these teachers by which higher-paid middle managers justify their jobs, even though there is not a shred of evidence that these overseers can make a dent in the problem of incompetent teachers.

But there are also healthier streams of discontent. Teachers in increasing numbers are signing up for summer work to increase their subject matter knowledge, pairing off in schools to observe and critique one another, forming little study groups, reaching out to do heroic work with families and communities, and working seriously at restructuring their schools for the purpose of improving their students' performance. These wholesome impulses are all leading to the creation of self-respecting faculty members who use their time to reflect on their own teaching and help one another improve.

A "Velvet Revolution" in Teaching

Increasing numbers of teachers are also struggling against the myriad obstacles to the improvement of their teaching. As more assertive teachers enter the ranks and begin to demand that their superiors support their efforts, the less assertive ones will become less timid, less tolerant of superiors who know less than they do, and less willing to live the lie that the schools are doing as well as can be expected, given what they have to work with.

Václav Havel, the spiritual and intellectual leader of Czechoslovakia's liberation from Communist domination, predicted fifteen years in advance of the event exactly how and why the Velvet Revolution would occur. The Communist dictatorship that so thoroughly demoralized the Czech people is not to be compared with the more benign and subtle domination of teachers by self-serving school bureaucracies, retrograde unions, and facile politicians in the United States. Nevertheless, there are thought-provoking parallels in this selection of quotations from Havel's writings:

> Life rebels against all uniformity and levelling; its aim is not sameness, but variety, the restlessness of transcendence, the adventure of novelty and rebellion against the status quo. An essential condition for its enhancement is the secret constantly made manifest.[11]

> If every day a man takes orders in silence from an incompetent superior, if every day he solemnly performs ritual acts which he privately finds ridiculous, if he unhesitatingly gives answers to questionnaires which are contrary to his real opinions and is prepared to deny his own self in public, if he sees no difficulty in feigning sympathy or even affection where, in fact, he feels only indifference and aversion, it still does not mean he has entirely lost the use of one of the basic human senses, namely the sense of *humiliation.*
>
> On the contrary, even if they never speak of it, people have a very acute appreciation of the price they have paid for outward peace and quiet; the permanent *humiliation of their human dignity.*[12]

> [But] since all genuine problems and matters of critical importance are hidden beneath a thick crust of lies, it is never quite clear when the proverbial last straw will fall, or what the straw will be.
>
> But the moment somebody breaks through in one place, when one person cries out, "The Emperor is naked!"—when a single person breaks the rules of the game, thus exposing the game—everything suddenly appears in another light and the whole crust seems then to be made of a tissue on the point of tearing and disintegrating uncontrollably.[13]

The conditions for a Velvet Revolution in teaching now exist. Teachers are increasingly conscious of assaults on their dignity and of disrespect for their knowledge. Aware of society's pressure on them to perform better, goaded by "choice" plans and other forms of competition, and closer to the woes of society's children than the rest of us are, teachers are increasingly turning to one another to seek ways of doing the one thing that satisfies them most—helping their students succeed.

There is a national consensus that traditional teacher education is inadequate, and that much more of the training of teachers should take place in the schools. But teachers know, even when their superiors do not, that few schools are up to that task. Teachers are struggling to define good practice so that they will be able to train novices. As they discover the ways in which trade-union commonplaces and contract provisions work against excellent training of novices, they are insisting that their unions address professional as well as bread-and-butter issues.

The incipient revolution in teaching and teacher education may be delayed if political leaders whip the public into a frenzy over vouchers, pit group against group in the competition for public resources, or capitulate to old-guard bureaucrats and union leaders. But these acts of political expediency will only sidetrack, not prevent, the eventual professionalization of teaching.

Any Future We Want

The United States is still relatively wealthy, and its people are vital, open to change, and eager for social and economic progress. As a society, we can have any future we want.

- We can continue to permit state legislatures to toy with teacher education according to the ebb and flow of special-interest pressures, or we can decide that a legislature is an improper venue for regulating professional training schools and hand the job over to NCATE, keeping a close watch on its work.
- We can continue to tolerate the licensing of unqualified teachers, which is part of what got us into our present mess, or we can decide not to tolerate that practice.

- We can continue to be cowed by university leaders who will not provide coherent, well-taught undergraduate programs in the arts and sciences for teachers, all the while whining about the unprepared graduates of the public schools, or we can insist, as taxpayers, that the universities get their priorities straight.
- We can continue to have fun complaining about stupid "methods" courses, or we can insist that professional studies for teachers be rigorous, coherent, and practical.
- We can continue as a society in which masses of adults have gone through the motions in school but are ahistorical and a-literate and spend much of their energy hiding their deficits in reading, writing, and mathematics, or we can have a society of adults who were taught to understand and apply what they learned in school to their personal, civic, and working lives.
- We can continue to tolerate school bureaucracies that treat teachers as automatons to carry out programs designed by distant superiors, or we can insist that public school leaders make maximum use of teachers' intelligence, experience, creativity, and commitment.
- We can continue to tolerate schools in which teachers are expected to teach for five or six unbroken hours and students are expected to sit still and concentrate for the same amount of time, or we can pay for a longer school day in which teachers have time to think and work together and students have time to relax and make friends in a wholesome and safe setting.

The teachers themselves will lead the way over the next decades. As citizens, our best strategy will be to patiently support the nation's teacher-leaders as they push through the encrusted layers of failed policies and wrong ideas.

NOTES

Preface

1. Murray, Frank B., and Fallon, Daniel. *The Reform of Teacher Education for the 21st Century: Project 30 One-Year Report.* Newark: College of Education, University of Delaware, 1980, pp. 6–7.
2. "Research About Teacher Education Project." American Association of Colleges of Teacher Education, *RATE V, Teaching Teachers: Facts and Figures.* Washington, D.C.: American Association of Colleges of Teacher Education, 1991, p. 38.

Chapter One

1. Silberman, Charles. *Crisis in the Classroom.* New York: Random House, 1970, p. 378.
2. Smith, Page. *Killing the Spirit.* New York: Penguin Books, 1990, p. 218.
3. Bok, Derek. *Higher Learning.* Cambridge, Mass.: Harvard University Press, 1986, p. 161.
4. Bishop, Beth A., and Anderson, Charles W. "Student Conceptions of Natural Selection and Its Role in Evolution." *Journal of Research in Science Teaching,* 1990, 27(5), 415–427.
5. Schoenfeld, Alan. "Metacognitive and Epistemological Issues in Mathematical Understanding." In E. A. Silver (ed.), *Teaching and Learning in Mathematical Problem Solving: Multiple*

Research Perspectives. Hillsdale, N.J.: Erlbaum, 1985, pp. 361–379.

6. Ball, Deborah. "Knowledge and Reasoning in Mathematical Pedagogy: Examining What Prospective Teachers Bring to Teacher Education." Unpublished doctoral dissertation, Michigan State University, 1988.

7. Borko, H., Brown, C., Underhill, R., Eisenhart, M., Jones, D., and Agard, P. *Learning to Teach Mathematics for Understanding.* College Park: University of Maryland, 1990.

8. Ball, D. "The Mathematical Understandings That Prospective Teachers Bring to Teacher Education." *Elementary School Journal,* 1990, *90*(4), 449–466.

9. McDiarmid, G. Williamson. *What Do Prospective Teachers Learn in Their Liberal Arts Courses?* East Lansing, Mich.: National Center for Research on Teacher Education, 1989.

10. Schrage, Michael. "If Statistics Are the Key to Quality, Our Students Need Some Chance Encounters." *Washington Post,* March 15, 1991, p. D3.

11. Anderson, C. W., and Roth, K. J. "Teaching for Meaningful and Self-Regulated Learning of Science." *Advances in Research on Teaching,* Vol. 1, 1989, pp. 265–309.

12. Hollon, R. E., and Anderson, C. W. Address to American Educational Research Association, Washington, D.C., Apr. 1987, p. 13.

13. Anderson and Roth, p. 274.

14. Silberman, p. 381.

15. Goodlad, John. *Teachers for Our Nation's Schools.* San Francisco: Jossey-Bass, 1990.

Chapter Two

1. Putka, G. "Making the Grade, Teaching Quality Rises with Improved Pay. Concern for Schools: How a School in San Antonio Lures a Phi Beta Kappa with Unusual Credentials." *Wall Street Journal,* Dec. 5, 1991, p. 1

2. At Hawthorne Elementary School, a subgroup of children is in a "collaborative" program, where the students stay together through the grades and are taught by teachers who have a

common philosophy. Last year's second graders in the program scored eight months ahead of the school second-grade average on the language-use sections of the Metropolitan Achievement Test. Math scores stayed the same.

Robert E. Lee High School established the Challenger programs for teens seen as likely to drop out. Their dropout rate fell to less than half of the districtwide average for at-risk students, and the students raised their grades above the school-wide average.

3. American Association of Colleges of Teacher Education, *RATE II, Teaching Teachers: Facts and Figures.* Washington D.C.: American Association of Colleges of Teacher Education, 1988.

4. Madeline Hunter is a well-known education consultant who developed a system of teaching a lesson. Her system, which is independent of content, is popular in many places and was adopted by several entire states, including Texas.

Chapter Five

1. Cross, K. Patricia. "The Rising Tide of School Reform Reports." *Phi Delta Kappan,* 1984, *66*(3), 167–172.

2. Parnell, Dale. *The Neglected Majority.* Washington, D.C.: American Association of Community and Junior Colleges, 1985.

3. National Center on Education and the Economy. *America's Choice: High Skills or Low Wages.* Report of the Commission on the Skills of the American Workforce. Rochester, N.Y.: National Center on Education and the Economy, 1990.

Chapter Seven

1. Watkins, B. "On California State U. Campuses, Everyone Is Responsible for Educating Teachers." *Chronicle of Higher Education,* Oct. 25, 1989, pp. A13–A15.

2. Bird, T., Anderson, Linda M., Sullivan, Barbara, and Swidler, Steve. "Pedagogical Balancing Acts: Problems Encountered in an Attempt to Influence Prospective Teachers' Beliefs about

Teaching Through an Introduction-to-Teaching Course."
Paper presented to the annual meeting of the American
Association of Colleges of Teacher Education, San Antonio,
Texas, Feb. 27, 1991, p. 10.

3. Bird, Anderson, Sullivan, and Swidler, p. 14.

Chapter Eight

1. Lieberman, Myron. *Education as a Profession.* Englewood
    Cliffs, N.J.: Prentice-Hall, 1956.

2. Conant, James B. *The Education of American Teachers.* New
    York: McGraw-Hill, 1963.

3. Koerner, James D. *The Miseducation of American Teachers.*
    Boston: Houghton Mifflin, 1965.

4. Goodlad, John. *Teachers for Our Nation's Schools.* San Fran-
    cisco: Jossey-Bass, 1990.

5. Smith, G. Pritchy. Address to symposium on recruiting mi-
    norities into teacher education, annual meeting of the Amer-
    ican Association of Teacher Educators, San Antonio, Texas,
    1992.

6. Smith, B. Othanel. *A Design for a School of Pedagogy.* Wash-
    ington, D.C.: U.S. Department of Education, 1980, p. 52.

7. Koerner, pp. 274–275.

8. Smith, B. Othanel, p. 52.

9. Wallace, Michelle. "Invisibility Blues." In Rich Simonson
    and Scott Walker (eds.), *Multicultural Literacy: Opening the
    American Mind.* Saint Paul, Minn.: Graywolf Press, 1988,
    p. 170.

10. Conant, p. 211.

Chapter Nine

1. Mosle, Sarah. "Scenes from the Class Struggle." *The New
    Republic,* Dec. 16, 1991, p. 27.

2. Murray, Frank B., and Fallon, Daniel. *The Reform of Teacher
    Education for the 21st Century: Project 30 One-Year Report.*
    Newark: College of Education, University of Delaware, 1980,
    pp. 7–8.

3. Sachar, Emily. "Teaching Doesn't Count." *The Washington Monthly*, Sept. 1990, pp. 24–25.
4. Stevenson, Harold W. "Learning from Asian Schools." *Scientific American*, Dec. 1992, *267*, 70–76.
5. Sizer, Theodore R. *Horace's Compromise: The Dilemma of the American High School*. Boston: Houghton Mifflin, 1984.
6. Stevenson, p. 13.
7. Stevenson, p. 13.

Chapter Ten

1. Olson, Lynn. "Reformers Seek to Untangle Web of Rules, Regulations to Improve Quality, Spark Innovation in Teacher Training." *Education Week*, Mar. 27, 1991, p. 12.
2. Olson, p. 13.
3. Goodlad, John. *Teachers for Our Nation's Schools*. San Francisco: Jossey-Bass, 1990, pp. 144–145.
4. Lyons, Gene. "Why Teachers Can't Teach." *Texas Monthly*, Sept. 1979, p. 128.
5. Haberman, Martin. "Catching Up with Reform in Teacher Education." *Education Week*, Nov. 6, 1991, p. 36.
6. Haberman, p. 29.
7. Wise, Arthur E. "Three Scenarios for the Future of Teaching." *Phi Delta Kappan*, 1986, *67*(9), 649–652.
8. Lyons, p. 128.
9. Kennedy, Mary M. *Generic and Curriculum-Specific Instructional Planning in Alternate Routes to Certification*. East Lansing: National Center for Research on Teacher Education, Michigan State University, 1990.
10. Toch, Thomas. *In the Name of Excellence*. New York: Oxford University Press, 1991, p. 102.

Chapter Eleven

1. Kearns, David T., and Doyle, Denis P. *Winning the Brain Race: A Bold Plan to Make Our Schools Competitive*. San Francisco: ICS Press, 1988.

2. Reich, Robert B. *The Work of Nations.* New York: Knopf, 1991, pp. 280–281.

3. Weisman, Jonathan. "Skills and Schools: Is Education Reform Just a Business Excuse?" *The Washington Post,* Mar. 29, 1992, pp. C1, C4.

4. Kozol, Jonathan. *Savage Inequalities.* New York: Crown, 1991.

5. Bomster, Mark. "Minn. Firm to Run 9 City Public Schools." *The Baltimore Sun,* June 10, 1992, p. 1.

6. Snider, William. "City Chiefs Eye Teacher Issues in Funding Context." *Education Week,* Oct. 12, 1988, p. 1.

7. Gursky, D. "Cincinnati Cuts More Than Half of Central Office." *Education Week,* May 20, 1992, p. 1.

8. Goodlad, John. *Teachers for Our Nation's Schools.* San Francisco: Jossey-Bass, 1990, p. 67.

9. Stempel, Amy Rukea. "BE [Council for Basic Education] Talks to Ted Sizer: The Politics of Reform." *Basic Education,* May 3, 1992, pp. 2–5.

10. Galbraith, John Kenneth. *The Culture of Contentment.* Boston: Houghton Mifflin, 1992, pp. 44–45.

11. Russakoff, D. "Lives Once Solid As Steel Shatter in Changed World." *The Washington Post,* April 13, 1991, p. 1.

12. Hornbeck, David W. "The True Road to Equity." *Education Week,* May 6, 1992, p. 32.

Chapter Twelve

1. La Rochefoucauld, "Maxims." In Evans, Bergen (ed.), *Dictionary of Quotations.* New York: Bonanza Books, 1968, p. 616.

2. Lockwood, Anne Turnbaugh (ed.). *Focus in Change.* Madison, Wis.: National Center for Effective Schools, 1990, p. 5.

3. Lockwood, p. 7.

4. Bradley, Ann. "Poll Finds Drop in Teachers' Satisfaction with Degree of Control over Their Jobs." *Education Week,* Sept. 5, 1990, p. 9.

5. Conley, David T. *Lessons from Laboratories in School Restructuring and Site-Based Decision-Making: Oregon's "2020"*

Schools Take Control of Their Own Reforms. Eugene: Oregon School Study Council, 1991, p. 34.

6. Transcript of Third "Tomorrow's Schools" Seminar, Michigan State University, Sept. 1989.

7. Sergiovanni, Thomas J. "Why We Should Seek Substitutes for Leadership." *Educational Leadership,* Feb. 1992, p. 43.

8. Sergiovanni, p. 41.

9. Brandt, Ron. "On Rethinking Leadership: A Conversation with Tom Sergiovanni." *Educational Leadership,* Feb. 1992, p. 46.

10. Rosiek, Jerry. "Training 'Subversives' as Teachers." *New York Times,* May 4, 1990, p. A25.

11. Havel, Václav. "Letter to Dr. Gustav Husak." In *Living in Truth.* London: Faber and Faber, 1986, pp. 23–24.

12. Havel, p. 31.

13. Havel, Václav. "The Power of the Powerless." In *Living in Truth,* p. 59.

INDEX

203